THE
SOVIET
HISTORY
OF
WORLD WAR II

Myths, Memories, and Realities

THE
SOVIET
HISTORY
OF
WORLD WAR II

Myths, Memories, and Realities

Matthew P. Gallagher

FREDERICK A. PRAEGER, *Publisher*
New York • London

FREDERICK A. PRAEGER, PUBLISHER
64 UNIVERSITY PLACE, NEW YORK 3, N.Y., U.S.A.
77–79 CHARLOTTE STREET, LONDON W.1, ENGLAND

Published in the United States of America in 1963 by
Frederick A. Praeger, Inc., Publisher

Second printing, 1963

Library of Congress Catalog Card Number: 63–9908

This book is Number 121 in the series of
Praeger Publications in Russian History and World Communism

Printed in the United States of America

To
ROBERTA
MY WIFE

Foreword

This book is aimed at illuminating an aspect of the Soviet past which has not been systematically examined before. Though it deals with the Soviet history of World War II, its principal subject is neither historiography nor military history. It is concerned primarily with the psychological and emotional conflicts generated within Soviet society by the mendacious account of the war given out in Soviet postwar propaganda. It is concerned secondarily with the official interpretations themselves, not for what they tell of the history of Soviet propaganda but for what they tell of the political and military history of the contemporary Soviet period.

In analyzing the reactions of Soviet people toward the postwar accounts of the war, this book focuses on three professional groups whose interests were most directly affected by official attitudes toward the war and whose views are revealed to the attentive reader of Soviet publications: the professional military, the historians, and the writers. A wide range of Soviet sources has been used to ascertain the currents of opinion entertained within these groups. Principal among these sources have been: for the military, the restricted-circulation General Staff publication, *Military Thought* (*Voyennaya Mysl'*); for the historians, the professional historical monthly, *Questions of History* (*Voprosy Istorii*); and for the writers, the literary press and certain literary journals. All offer distinctive advantages for the purposes of this study. *Military Thought* provided a forum for military officers to discuss wartime experience with some freedom from propaganda prescriptions.

Questions of History published some legitimate research as well as propaganda, and like other journals of its kind afforded some insights into currents of opinion within the professional community by the accounts of historical meetings that it carried. The literary journals, because of their relative editorial autonomy, could exercise some latitude in interpreting the limits of official tolerance— a fact that sometimes permitted fresh and nonpolitical views to be expressed.

The account of Soviet writings on the war is presented here in terms of the issues created by the early postwar distortions. The starting point of this study is the wartime period in which the concerns, tensions, and moments of truth of that experience filtered through into the contemporary reportage. Its central portion is the Stalinist postwar period in which the demands of Stalin's vanity, and the political goals of the Party, defined the contents of the official history of the war. Its concluding portion is the period since Stalin's death, in which many of the distortions introduced by Stalin were corrected and the official version of the war brought closer to the truth. This book does not provide a comprehensive account of current Soviet historiography on the war.

Although this has been a solitary and—within its modest limits —a pioneering study, I am thoroughly aware of the debt I owe to others. I think I owe most to people whom I do not know—to the scholars who have gone before and charted many of the paths through the still poorly explored area of Soviet postwar literature. I owe much also to others to whom I was a stranger when I first approached them. I wish to mention Miss Vera Alexandrova, in particular, who offered me leads to material she herself had not had time to use. Professors Alexander Dallin and Cyril E. Black responded with equal generosity, the former with detailed bibliographical suggestions, the latter with a critique of my original plan of research.

I wish to thank also Dr. Sherman Kent, of whom I can say with literal accuracy that his assistance made this work possible;

Mr. Set Mardirosian, whose knowledge and imagination has been for me a constant source of insights into the Soviet system; Professor Richard Pipes, who guided me in my doctoral dissertation, which is the basis of this book; Dr. Raymond L. Garthoff, who over the past few years has given me generously of his unparalleled knowledge in this field and who read and commented upon the draft of an earlier version of this book.

Finally, I wish to record my debt to my family: to my wife, for her unfailing solicitude and quiet skill, which created the environment necessary for this work; and to my children, Matthew, Robert, and Paula, who cheerfully made adjustments in their lives to accommodate my needs.

Acknowledgment

A substantial portion of the last chapter is based on a paper delivered by the author at a conference on Soviet historiography held in Geneva on July 16–23, 1961, under the joint auspices of *Survey* and the Institut Universitaire des Hautes Etudes Internationales. The author and publisher are indebted to the Editors of *Survey* for their kind permission to reprint the material in question.

Contents

Introduction

It is a paradox of Soviet history that events that loom the largest in the popular memory cast the shortest shadows in the official histories of the regime. One looks in vain in Soviet sources for accounts of the famines of the post–Civil War years, the collectivization drive against the peasants, or the purges of the 1930's. These are, as the Russian people say, "white spots" in the official textbooks—unwritten pages that testify to events the regime wishes to leave in obscurity.

Until recent years, World War II was such a white spot in Soviet history. Stalin's wartime writings and speeches collected in the volume *The Great Patriotic War of the Soviet Union* constituted for many years the only official history of the war. A smattering of books and pamphlets and an intermittent trickle of newspaper and journal articles completed the historical record. After Stalin's death, the record expanded—first through criticisms of the distortions and omissions of the Stalinist propaganda, then by new writings that gradually repaired the earlier defaults. Much progress has now been made, but it comes some fifteen years after an event that in any other society would have absorbed the efforts of a generation of historians, writers, and military specialists. And it was made possible only by a political convulsion that itself attested to the strength of the taboos that had been erected around all aspects of the Stalinist past, including the history of the war.

The long official reticence about the history of the war was understandable. No event cut more deeply across the fabric of Soviet history or left larger gaps for the official historians to repair than World War II. In a dozen different ways the war was an embarrassment for the Soviet Union. The pact with Hitler, the failure to anticipate and prepare for the German invasion, the forced retreats, the losses of huge territories and populations—all would have defied ready explanation by a democratic government, let alone by a regime with such overweening pretensions to foresight and infallibility.

Equally awkward were the statements and actions that registered the compromises and expedients forced upon the regime by wartime necessity. The anti-Hitler coalition itself was a heavy legacy—complicated by the generous assessments that the regime had given of the Western Allies' contribution to the victory. Worse still were the friendly gestures that had been made to the people. "My friends," Stalin had addressed the people in his first speech after the invasion. The far-reaching implications of this single phrase—the impact it carried within the Soviet Union—is conveyed through the insight of the novelist. A scene in the novel *The Living and the Dead* depicts a wounded soldier lying in a hospital bed amidst the groans of his dying companions, "pondering every detail of the speech of Stalin and the spirit of appeal that permeated it. 'My friends'—the phrase was repeated again and again the next day throughout the whole hospital."[1]

Thus, the writing of the history of the war involved more than the whitewashing of mistakes and miscalculations, more than the rationalization of unseemly alliances. For the Stalinist regime, it involved the disavowal of the tacit promise it had given that from the common enterprise of the war a new life would emerge for the Soviet people, a life in which they could expect peace in the world and the respect of their own government. The interpretation of the war disseminated by Soviet propagandists during the postwar period was one of the most audacious efforts ever undertaken by the Soviet leadership to tailor history to political prescription. Even without direct evidence on the effect of this propaganda on

the Soviet population, it would be hard to believe that distortions
of the kind involved in this interpretation, touching matters that
broad elements of the population had experienced at first hand,
could have been carried off without some degree of internal resentment and resistance. Ordinary citizens who had borne the brunt
of the leaders' mistakes, literary figures whose craft demanded
respect for the truth, military men who had a personal and professional stake in a true record of the war, even purveyors of propaganda who were unprepared for the swift hardening of the official
climate—all must have felt at least an inertial resistance to the
imposition of the official line.

One wonders about the silent appraisals that were made as the
people listened to the propaganda assurances that what they had
seen with their own eyes had not in fact taken place, that throughout the war the leadership had remained always in confident control, that all had taken place according to plan. The insight of the
novelist again provides the surest guide to the popular mind.
Simonov explores the quandary of the "two truths" as it presented
itself to a wartime military correspondent. His hero, the correspondent, after a harrowing week of narrow escapes from death
and captivity, is asked by his editor if he has any "material" to
report. The correspondent considers the implications of the question. He has seen more during the past week than he has seen in
a lifetime. But can it be printed? The official radio communiqué
was at that very moment reporting huge battles along the borders,
yet he, just three days back, had been unable to get even as far
as Minsk. Which should he believe—the communiqué, or what
he had seen with his own eyes? Could there be two truths? But
even if this were possible, the newspaper could print only one—
"the single truth!" Finally, after a long silence, looking the editor
straight in the eye, he responds: "No, I have no material." And—
the novelist points out—"they both understood each other."[2]

While the ordinary people remained silent, those who had access
to the public print—historians, writers, and military specialists—

were in a position to give some voice to their views. The story of
the conduct of these individuals during the harsh postwar days
when the official line was being imposed, their persistent and often
lonely battles against official pressure, and their vigorous espousal
of truth when this was possible, constitutes the principal subject
of this book. It is a story that is both exciting and reassuring, for
it gives evidence that beneath the artificial calm of Soviet society
men thought and acted—and continue to think and act—according
to universal values beyond the regime's powers to proscribe.

This book tells another story as well—the story of the gradual
acceptance by the regime of the concept of the utility of historical
truth. In this one field of history, at least, some genuine progress
has been made toward providing an account of what really happened. This progress has been nurtured and sustained by practical
necessity. Recognizing that some scope for historical truth was
needed to encourage the vigor and integrity of military thought
required by contemporary military realities, the regime has loosened
the reins on military historians to restudy World War II experience. However expedient this marriage of utility and truth may be,
it is for us a happy union, for it has given birth to a historical
activity that is now beginning to provide, for the first time, a Soviet
contribution to the history of World War II.

THE
SOVIET
HISTORY
OF
WORLD WAR II

Myths, Memories, and Realities

1

The Historical Issues and the Wartime Record

The tensions and conflicts that have surrounded the history of the war in the Soviet Union had their origins in the alterations of history carried out by Soviet propagandists during the early postwar period. These alterations, aimed at inflating the Stalin image and at denigrating the Western nations, affected four major areas of the history of the war. First, and most important, because it violated the personal experience of many millions of the Soviet people, was the attempt to absolve the Soviet leadership from any responsibility for the early defeats and to explain the initial retreats of the Soviet Army as dictated by a strategy that had been worked out beforehand; second, was the effacement of the soldiers and ordinary people from the history of the war and the arrogation to Stalin and the Party of all the credits for the victory; third, was the discrediting of the motives and performance of the Western Allies in the war; and, fourth—an issue of interest mainly to historians—was the interpretation of the Japanese surrender as stemming from Soviet intervention rather than from the cumulative punishment of American military pressure culminating in the atomic bombings.

These interpretations of history were at variance not only with the facts in each case but also with the account of these facts that

3

the Soviet Government had been willing to give its people during the war. Not all of the people were in a position to know the facts. But some were. And others were at least capable of recognizing the discrepancies between the newer and older versions of the same events. In this chapter, an attempt is made to suggest the standards of comparison that were available to the Soviet people as the postwar propaganda campaign opened. Each of the areas of the history of the war mentioned above is presented under three aspects: first, as the events in question actually happened; second, as they were interpreted in the postwar propaganda; and third, as they had been presented to the people during the war itself.

THE INITIAL PERIOD OF THE SOVIET-GERMAN WAR

In a political sense, the war began for the Soviet Union at the time the threat of German aggression began to dominate the direction and pace of Soviet foreign and domestic policies. By this calendar, the Soviet Union's entry into the war was belated, and her leaders showed themselves to be as spendthrift of opportunities for timely opposition to Hitler and—when these opportunities had passed—almost as laggard in preparing for war as the leaders of the Western states. Viewing the world through a glass darkened by ideological prejudices, they were unable to appreciate the sincerity of the Western states' opposition to Hitler and disdained to make the accommodations necessary to bring this moral force into play on their own behalf. The capitulation at Munich, to be sure, was a Western blunder, and it is doubtful, given the personality of Chamberlain, that any actions the Soviet Union might have taken could have prevented it. But Munich did not present the last chance to block Hitler's aggression.

During the spring and summer of 1939, a series of negotiations took place between the Western states and the Soviet Union aimed at arranging joint guarantees against further German expansion in eastern Europe. Much has been written about Western culpability for the failure of this diplomatic effort, but there was blame to share by all. If the Soviet leaders ever put stock in the feasibility and desirability of joint action with the West at this juncture, their expectations in this direction were short-lived, and from very early in the negotiations they took care to prepare an alternative line. In April, the Soviet Union began to take soundings in Berlin as to the possibility of achieving a *modus vivendi* with Germany.[1] From that time on, Soviet policy began to probe for a German understanding, and while the British and French pressed more anxiously for some arrangement in the East, the Russians placed increasingly unacceptable conditions in the way of agreement. Finally, in the summer of 1939, while an Anglo-French military mission was actually in Moscow working for an understanding with the Soviet Union, the Soviet-German nonaggression pact was concluded.

The nonaggression pact with Germany, negotiated behind the backs of the English and French—and at their expense—won for the Soviet Union a year and a half of grace to prepare for the eventual clash with Germany. In some respects, the Soviet Union used this period to advantage. It participated in the partition of Poland, extending its western border approximately to the old Curzon Line, tore Karelia from Finland as spoils of the winter war of 1939–40, and absorbed the Baltic states and Bessarabia in 1940. In this way it erected a buffer zone between itself and Germany. In the sphere of internal military preparations, it was less successful. As early as 1937, the Soviet Union had begun a program to replace its obsolete military equipment, but this program was not pursued with the vigor the situation required, and military units did not begin to get the new weapons until the very eve of the war.[2] Likewise, although the expansion of the army had begun before the war, border-troop units were not placed on a war footing. The most reliable Soviet account of this period states: "A significant number of the divisions comprising the garrison of the border districts were made up of contingents newly called up on the eve of the war, the majority of which had not received even minimal training in using the complex military equipment comprising the armament of the troops."[3] According to the same source, the rifle divisions on the immediate border defenses were maintained at peacetime strength (12,000 men), but those behind the lines were maintained at reduced peacetime strength (6,000 men).

These disadvantages were compounded by political mistakes. There is ample evidence that the Soviet Government was fully informed of the German intention to attack long before the invasion took place. Churchill has described the careful personal efforts he made to bring the seriousness of the situation to Stalin's attention.[4] He has also told of other warnings conveyed to the Soviet Government by subordinate British officials and the American Government.[5] And investigations after the war revealed that Soviet spy networks in Austria and Japan had also uncovered advance information on the German invasion plans.[6] Finally, Khrushchev, in his secret speech to the Twentieth Party Congress, cited many additional indications that had been made available to the Soviet Government through its own diplomatic and military sources.[7] All of these warnings were discounted by Stalin as stemming from Western provocative maneuvers, and, far from acting in the light of them, he contributed further to disarming the vigilance of the country by publicly announcing, in a Tass statement of June 14, that rumors of an impending attack were groundless. In addition, to avoid giving the Germans any pretext for hostilities, most divisions of the border screen were ordered to keep only one of their regiments on the border, while their main forces were held in camps or military towns 8 to 20 kilometers behind the front.[8]

German accounts of the first period of the war confirm this picture of political blindness and military unpreparedness on the Soviet side. General Guderian, the German tank leader, has told about his observations of the Soviet front lines just before the attack began, which showed that the Soviet troops were completely unaware of the impending danger.

On the 20th and 21st, I visited the forward units of my corps to make sure that all preparations for the attack were satisfactorily completed. Detailed study of the behavior of the Russians convinced me that they knew nothing of our intentions. We had observation of the courtyard of the Brest-Litovsk citadel and could see them drilling by platoons to the music of a military band. The strong points along their bank of the Bug were unoccupied. They had made scarcely any noticeable progress in strengthening their fortifications during the past few weeks.[9]

On June 22, 1941, three German Army groups that had been stealthily deployed in East Prussia and Poland crashed into the fragile shield of the Soviet border defenses, achieving complete tactical surprise. Soviet planes were caught on the ground at their airfields and were largely destroyed. Even after the invasion had begun, Stalin refused to believe the reports that came pouring in, and the staffs of the border districts received orders to assume full alert status the morning of the first day of fighting.[10] By this time, it was obviously too late to conduct any effective resistance, even with the inadequate resources on hand. The first step of the blitzkrieg, the piercing of the front, had been achieved.

In the following days, the German armored columns raced into the interior at record speeds. In the north, Manstein's Panzer corps seized a bridgehead across the Dvina, 200 miles from the border, in just four days of fighting,[11] and within eighteen days, the northern army had penetrated the borders of Leningrad Province. In the center, Guderian's tanks emerged in the vicinity of Smolensk by mid-July. At the same time, the advance armor of Rundstedt's southern group had come up to the outer defenses of Kiev. In all, during the first three weeks of the war, the German armies achieved a tempo of advance of 25 miles per day and penetrated up to 500 miles into the Soviet interior.

Here the German advance paused, not only because of Russian resistance, but because of cross-purposes in the German High Command. Hitler wished to divert the tank armies from the Moscow direction to assist in the flank attacks on Leningrad and Kiev, while the German generals wished to continue the advance on the central front. The generals vainly temporized and in the end acquiesced to Hitler's decision, meanwhile letting many weeks of the best campaigning weather slip away. By the end of August, the main objective of the German advance was shifted to the south, where two armies from the central front were sent to assist in the liquidation of the Russian southern wing. A huge encirclement around Kiev resulted in the capture of more than 500,000 Soviet troops.[12] Finally, on October 2, the advance on Moscow was resumed, but by the time the first successes around Vyazma had been consolidated, the fall slush had set in. Slowed to a crawl by the weather and the stiffening Russian resistance, the advance finally petered out a few miles from Moscow and was then mauled back by the Soviet counteroffensive that began on December 6.

The retreat of the Soviet Army during the summer and fall of 1941 was conditioned by the political mistakes made on the eve of the war and by the command failures during the course of the retreat itself. Deprived of airpower and large mobile reserves, and bound by the Supreme Command strategy of defending "each inch of native soil," the army repeatedly permitted large forces to be encircled where a more flexible strategy might have saved them. From July 10, the defensive front was divided into three main commands: the Northwestern, under Marshal Voroshilov; the Western, under Marshal Timoshenko; and the Southwestern, under Marshal Budennyy. These old Bolsheviks proved themselves incapable of coping with the new conditions of warfare created by the deep German penetrations of prepared defense positions. At times, command leadership collapsed completely, as in the catastrophic rout at Kiev. Even the Soviet source quoted earlier admits the scale of this failure. "The Command of the Southwestern front was unable to organize the leadership of the military operations of the encircled troops. Direction of the troops was lost, and the withdrawal from the encirclement took place in an extremely disorganized manner by separate groups and units."[13] On October 19,

General Zhukov took over command of the Western front, and thereafter Soviet resistance hardened. This was due partly to the narrowing of the arc of defense as the German advance approached Moscow, which permitted the Russians to concentrate superior forces at the threatened points; but it was due also to the imaginative use of these forces by Zhukov.

The behavior of the Soviet troops themselves was uneven. Many German generals have commented on the staunch fighting qualities displayed by individual Soviet soldiers, but others have remarked on their peculiar dependence upon firm leadership and control. When the command structure collapsed, as in the early days of the war, many units were unable to improvise effective resistance. The huge bag of prisoners taken by the Germans during the first year of the war, which reached 2 million men at least,* testifies to the existence of a large-scale morale crisis in the Soviet Union at that time. Hints of its existence are scattered in Soviet war literature and implied in certain wartime acts of the Soviet Government, such as the decree against spies and diversionists[14] and the restoration of the commissar system in the army.[15] One careful study of an episode in this phenomenon, the October crisis in Moscow, shows that public defeatism at times reached epidemic proportions.[16]

The reasons for the final failure of the German offensive are many and largely of German origin. An important factor has been mentioned—the conflicts between Hitler and the generals—which in turn reflected the excessiveness of the demands that Hitler had imposed upon his forces. By the time of the final German advance

* Estimates of the number of military prisoners taken by the Germans vary considerably, for the Soviet Government has never provided precise data on this subject. The above figure is arrived at by adding up the German claims for the four largest encirclements of 1941 alone, those at Minsk, Smolensk, Kiev, and Vyazma. These figures are frequently cited by Western military authorities, and the total estimate of 2 million prisoners appears to be compatible with the Soviet wartime propaganda acknowledgment of 4.5 million total casualties (including wounded) suffered during the first year of the war.

on Moscow, German forces were overextended, both in terms of logistic communications and in the ratio of operational reserves to committed forces. Men and machines were exhausted from the long summer campaigns and the shifting of armies from one front to another over a great territorial expanse. Before the beginning of the Russian campaign, German divisions had been thinned out to spread the available manpower and armor among the 146 divisions participating in the invasion.[17] This gave them relative superiority during the early period of the war, particularly after the initial surrenders of Soviet troops; but this advantage was certainly lost by the end of the year. Finally, the cold weather that came on early and rapidly in 1941 caught the Germans unprepared, because, anticipating a lightning victory, they had not adapted their machines and weapons to winter operations or even provided winter clothing for the troops.

Since the stopping of the German offensive before Moscow marks a natural turning point in the course of the war, it will be appropriate to conclude our review at this point and turn to a consideration of the account of these events that was given in Soviet postwar propaganda.

In general, Soviet postwar propaganda ignored or denied the political and military failures of the first year of the war. Soviet propaganda made no acknowledgment, for example, that the Soviet Union had ever received any advance warning of the German intention to attack. Instead, it sought to turn to advantage the blunder that the Soviet Government had committed in discounting these warnings. It depicted the Soviet Union as the victim of German "perfidy," it stressed the "suddenness" of the German attack. The initial defeats were presented as flowing from the natural disadvantage suffered by a peace-loving state in the face of a ruthless aggressor. At the same time, the prewar policies of the Soviet Union, its industrialization programs, and its diplomatic and military encroachments in eastern Europe were presented as calculated against an eventual German attack, and thus as responsible for the country's ability to withstand the shock when the attack came.

As for the great retreats of the first year, Soviet postwar propaganda sought to portray them as the preliminary stages of victory. A picture was presented of the Soviet Supreme Command as being in masterly control of the situation at all times and as manipulating the course of events. The strategy of the Supreme Command, it was said, was one of winning time and, by "exhausting and bleeding white" the enemy, to prepare the ground for a successful counteroffensive.

There were two formulas in Soviet postwar propaganda that were very important in the official account of the early World War II period and that express the whole tenor of this account. The first was the so-called strategy of active defense, which was represented as a Supreme Command plan embracing not only the tactical methods of aggressive counteraction in defense but the whole strategic conception of the early period of Soviet operations. The second and more important formula was the so-called strategic counteroffensive, which also was said to embrace, as parts of a preconceived plan, the whole complex of defensive actions conducted by the Soviet Army preliminary to the launching of the actual counteroffensive.

The morale crisis that gripped the Soviet Army and people in 1941 was handled more simply—Soviet postwar propaganda simply ignored it. The morale of the Soviet troops, and of the Soviet population in general, was presented as unexampled, and every event, good or bad, was hailed as contributing "still further to the monolithic unity" of the country.

Even the positive achievements of the first year of the war were idealized and distorted in Soviet postwar propaganda. The stopping of the German advance before Moscow was claimed as a triumph of Soviet strategy, and all accidental factors and German mistakes were discounted. German logistic problems and leadership conflicts, although discussed occasionally in general disparagement of German strategy and military science, were never admitted as decisive factors. The weather was mentioned in Soviet accounts, but only as interfering with Soviet operations. The manpower relationship was always claimed to be in the German favor, and the 170 German and 38 satellite divisions attributed to the German invasion force by the Russians during the war was the figure retained in subsequent accounts. In short, any factor that tended to diminish the achievements of the Soviet leadership and Army for stopping the German invasion was ignored in Soviet postwar propaganda.

This Soviet historical account of the first period of the war, which was characterized chiefly by its attempt to impute foresight and planning to the conduct of the Soviet Army during the forced retreat, bore little resemblance to the chaotic conditions that actually obtained. How does this interpretation compare with the account that the regime gave out during the wartime period itself?

The basic outlines of this interpretation were clearly present in the wartime accounts. This was natural, since the guidelines of wartime censorship were similar in their effect to the political goals of postwar policy. Thus, whether to encourage morale during the war or to enhance leadership prestige after the war, events tended to be presented in the rosiest possible colors. Apart from this, there were also notable differences. These appeared in the general spirit of the wartime accounts, as well as in certain details that showed that wartime censorship was less sensitive to leadership pretensions to infallibility than the postwar ideological censorship came to be.

The most characteristic feature of the wartime accounts was the sense of partnership they implied between the regime and the people. Stalin appeared as the leader, as the organizer of desperate measures, as the head of the government and army, as the genius commander. But he was not yet the manipulator of events. The responsibility of leadership was somewhat diffused; each element of the population was shown playing its vital and necessary role. The desperate defensive battles of the first part of the war did not yet appear as mere preliminaries to an ultimate and preordained victory.

During the war, nothing was heard about the strategy of the counteroffensive. The term "active defense" appeared occasionally in the accounts of this period, but not with the meaning of a pre-arranged strategy and not as a major propaganda device. It was a descriptive term, well suited to the purposes of Soviet propaganda and intended to convey the impression that Soviet troops were putting up a stubborn resistance to German pressure. The substance of the concept appeared more often than the actual phrase itself, in frequent references to "mobile defense," "active operations," the "activeness" of Soviet tactics, etc.[18] Later in the war, the term began to take on the meaning of a strategic concept as a result of Stalin's May Day speech of 1942, which implied that the early defensive battles had won time for the constantly operating factors of war to come into play.[19] But its full flowering as a major interpretive device of the first period of the war did not take place until later.

The impression that events were taking their own course and that the activities of the Soviet leadership were being defined by rather than defining the course of events was reinforced by the concentration of Soviet propaganda of the time on the initiative and independence of ordinary Soviet citizens and soldiers. The innumerable stories of war heroism played up the role of individuals and small units in improvising resistance to the Germans. Stalin himself gave an impetus to this emphasis in his radio speech of July 3, calling for all-out partisan war on the invaders. Thereafter, stories of partisan exploits began to appear in the Soviet press with increasing frequency. The same emphasis was often placed on the activities of regular military units. One prominent military writer summed up the general character of much of this writing— giving, incidentally, an unintended insight into the tenuousness of central command at the time—when he acclaimed "the independence and initiative displayed by Soviet units—large or small—when thrown on their own resources."[20]

Hints that German difficulties and miscalculations played a part in the final outcome of the campaign also appeared in the wartime accounts. One of the first historical résumés of the 1941 campaign by a qualified military writer contained a number of such admissions. It implied rather broadly, for example, that the manpower ratio had shifted against the Germans by the time of the final thrust on Moscow. "As the whole subsequent course of the struggle showed," it said, "the Germans had miscalculated. They had underestimated the forces of opposition of the Red Army, its deep and numerous reserves."[21] It also stressed the logistic problems of the Germans, with their communications "stretched over 1,000 kilometers and under the blows of the partisans and aviation."[22] Finally, it mentioned the weather. "Soldiers and officers taken prisoner by us presented a pitiable sight. Clothed in summer uniforms, frozen, often wrapped in scarves and muffled in fur jackets and women's coats stolen from the local population, they reminded one strongly of the remnants of the French Army in 1812 retreating from Moscow to the western border."[23]

Acknowledgments of failures and mistakes on the Soviet part also appeared during the war, particularly in Stalin's wartime speeches. They were full of indirect references to the morale crisis that gripped the Soviet Union during the first months of the war. Stalin urged a ruthless fight against all "disorganizers of the rear, deserters, panicmongers, rumormongers." He disputed the defeatism of "terror-stricken would-be intellectuals." He acknowledged "complacency and frivolousness with regard to the enemy . . . among Red Army men in the first months of the patriotic war." Stalin's speeches also contained implicit admissions that military operations did not always redound to the credit of the Soviet Army. He spoke of the Army and Navy in 1941 as "still young," and "not yet . . . professional," and he later described the initial retreats as "forced."[24] Finally, in his victory toast to the Russian people, he stated flatly that the retreats of the Russian Army during the first period of the war took place "because there was no other way out."[25]

In sum, whereas the wartime accounts contained the distortions and exaggerations common to this genre of literature in all countries, they also contained hints that the war had been something less than a triumphant promenade.

CREDITS FOR THE VICTORY

Thus far we have considered mainly the blacker days of the war and the way in which Soviet propaganda touched up, and then distorted, the embarrassing facts of that experience. Let us now turn to another side of the wartime experience, the winning of the victory. In its most important aspect for Soviet postwar propaganda, this question involved the issue of which of the four pillars of Soviet wartime society—the Army, the Party, the people, or Stalin alone—deserved the laurels of victory and, hence, the rewards and prerogatives that they symbolized.

Before considering the merits of the claims that could be advanced for the several candidates, and the way in which the credits were in fact allotted, it will be useful to review in summary fashion the course of the war from the point where we left it at the end of 1941. The end of the Soviet winter offensive, which had begun before Moscow, was signalized by the liquidation of the brief Soviet lodgment on the Kerch Peninsula in mid-May, 1942, and the turning of Timoshenko's Kharkov offensive into a disastrous trap at the end of that month. Shortly thereafter, the German summer offensive, aimed at the oil resources of the Caucasus and entailing a cut across the Russian north-south communications at Stalingrad, began with initial successes comparable to those of 1941. Presumably to justify the strategy of husbanding reserves north of the German drive, and perhaps also to invigorate the will to resist,

Stalin later announced that the German offensive into the Caucasus was essentially a diversionary maneuver and that the basic German plan was to strike across the Volga and thence north, to encircle Moscow from the rear. In retrospect, this magnified the significance of the Stalingrad victory, although in actual fact the victory needed no embellishment. The Germans reached Stalingrad in September, fought their way into the city, and penetrated to the Volga in several places. After a tense period of fighting, in which the Germans failed to dislodge the Russians from the bluffs along the river or to silence the Russian batteries across the river, the siege settled down to a military stalemate. By this time, the German generals were aware of the threat to their flanks, which were covered in large part by unreliable Rumanian divisions, but Hitler, fearing the consequences to his prestige, refused to permit withdrawal. The Russian counteroffensive that began north and south of the German wedge in November was aimed at squeezing the Germans out of Stalingrad,[26] but when the Germans neglected to withdraw, it was turned into a trap. The result was the end of the German 6th Army, including the loss by surrender of its commanding general, Marshal von Paulus. This success led to the retreat of the Germans from the Caucasus, where their position was now untenable, and to the retrieval by the Russians of the ground lost during the summer. A last great offensive bid was initiated by the Germans in July, 1943, at Kursk, but it ground itself to pieces on the well-prepared Russian defenses. Thereafter, the Russian offensive gained momentum, reaching the right-bank Ukraine by the end of 1943, developing in 1944 into what Soviet propaganda described as the "ten Stalinist crushing blows," and in 1945 into the final assault on Berlin.

With this brief introduction, it will now be appropriate to turn to the contributions of the various elements of Soviet society to this course of events and the treatment accorded them in Soviet propaganda. Let us start with Stalin, since his figure loomed largest in Soviet postwar accounts.

Just what Stalin's role was in the strategic direction of the Soviet Army is not entirely clear. Khrushchev's account, in his secret speech, of the telephone calls he made to Vasilevskiy and Malenkov at the time of the Kharkov battle establishes the fact that Stalin exercised at least a general supervision over military operations.[27] It is probable that his dictatorial habits and affectations of military competence led him to interfere more directly in military matters than the other Allied leaders commonly permitted themselves to do. But in the actual conception and direction of military operations, he was probably cautious enough to limit his interference to the confirmation or veto of plans presented by General Headquarters. Even within these limits, and judging by the bits of evidence available, his record as a war leader was far from consistently good. His gross error in discounting the numerous intelligence indications of the German preparations for attack has been mentioned above. His strategy of "no retreat" during the first period of the war played into the hands of the German encirclement tactics, and his stubborn insistence on continuing the Kharkov offensive in 1942 after the Soviet position had become hopeless was, to say the least, militarily unjustified. His competence for command was apparently also negatively affected by his moodiness of character. Khrushchev charged that Stalin became panic-stricken in 1941,[28] and Churchill's account of Stalin's desperate appeal for a British expeditionary corps at that time lends corroboration to this charge.[29]

In postwar propaganda, however, Stalin was transformed into the "greatest commander of all ages." All military operations were said to have been carried out according to his plans and under his immediate direction. He was said to have "worked out anew" and, for the first time in history, to have applied with full effect the "strategic counteroffensive" that constituted the greatest contribution ever made in the annals of military science. This hyperbole will

perhaps be sufficient to suggest the direction taken by Soviet official propaganda on Stalin's role in the war. It went well beyond the
image of Stalin that had been sponsored during the war itself, although Stalinist glorification reached large dimensions at that time,
too. The American correspondent Walter Kerr, in his account of
his wartime adventures in Russia, illustrated this in an amusing
description of a luncheon with Marshal Malinovskiy at which the
Marshal tirelessly arose to amend each toast with an appropriate
accolade to Stalin.[30] The essential difference between the wartime
and postwar attitudes was that in the former, Stalin's figure had not
yet blotted out the other contributors to the victory.

The army was the group that suffered most directly from the
postwar inflation of the Stalin image. The record of the professional military leaders during the war was good. Whatever their
merits when compared with their opposite numbers in the West—
and there are differences of opinion on this score—they were the
men who bore the responsibility for military decisions, and they
were the men who stood at the head of the troops when victory was
achieved. Moreover, their contribution was opportune and dramatic. It was after Zhukov took over from the old Bolshevik Timoshenko as commander in chief of the Western front[31] that Moscow
was saved and the first Soviet counteroffensive successfully carried
out. It was also after Zhukov took over as *Stavka* representative on
the Southern fronts and after the commissar system had been
abolished in the army, that Stalingrad was saved and the series of
operations launched that led to ultimate victory.[32] The figure of
Zhukov in these key events of the war was symbolic of the professional military's role in rescuing the regime from the consequences
of its own incompetence.

In postwar propaganda, the marshals rapidly faded into the
background. Zhukov's fall from honor has often been noted. It was
so swift and complete that the Soviet press observed the first anniversary of the fall of Berlin without mentioning his name. The
articles published on the occasion of Stalin's seventieth birthday,

in 1949, performed the equally remarkable feat of reviewing the
whole course of the war without naming a single Soviet general
officer. This ignominy, of course, contrasted sharply with the recognition that had been accorded the military leaders during the war
itself. It could not be said that at that time they actually vied with
Stalin for honor—he was always unapproachable in this respect—
but at least they appeared clearly in the background. Lieutenant
General Shilovskiy provides a fairly typical example of the way in
which the relationship of Stalin with the marshals was expressed
at that time:

Here [before Moscow], the Stalinist genius for foresight and wise leadership, the great patriotism of the Soviet people, and the courage and
skill of the Red Army merged into one and became an insurmountable
obstacle for the enemy. The plan for the destruction of the enemy,
pointed out by Comrade Stalin, was brilliantly realized on the Western
front under the leadership of General of the Army Zhukov.[33]

One effect of such formulas, it will be seen, was to make the
marshals stand out in sharper relief by the very mistiness of the
Olympian heights to which Stalin was assigned.

The Party's role in the war is perhaps the most difficult to
evaluate. It was so closely woven into the fabric of Soviet society
that it is hard now to distinguish, through the smoke screen of
propaganda raised on its behalf, where Party inspiration left off
and public initiative began in the great social and military achievements of the war. Unquestionably, the Party's traditional role as
the leader and coordinator of national energies was diminished
during the war as increasing reliance came to be placed on non-
Party channels of public control and extraordinary governmental
and military bodies arose to take over direction of the war effort.
To name merely the one activity that the Party later claimed most
vigorously for its own credit—the partisan movement—the facts
seem to be that the Party had little to do with organizing the
movement, and that it established control later only with difficulty

and never with full effectiveness.[34] In general, the conclusion seems safe that among the instruments available to the Soviet leadership for conducting the war effort, the Party apparatus performed an auxiliary function.

This conclusion is confirmed in part by the relative backstaging of the Party and its principles in the public stance of the Soviet leadership during the war. An index of this relative effacement was the virtual absence in Stalin's wartime speeches of references to the Party's activities in the war. In his public activities, he associated himself more closely with the government and the army than with the Party and acted as prime minister or as head of the State Defense Committee or as commander in chief, and, when addressing the people, he spoke on behalf of the government first and the Party second. Many of the public attitudes that had provided the setting and rationale of Party activities in the past were relegated to the background. Appeals were made over the head of the socialist tradition, as it were, to the historical sources of Russia's national patriotism; friendly relations were established with the Church; the Comintern was abolished. However disingenuous this public attitude may have been, however much calculated for effect in the West, it cannot have failed to have an effect on the public understanding of leadership beliefs and intentions.

Finally, we must note the role of the people in the war. Their contribution had been so massive, and so clearly affirmed by the regime during the war, that it stood in the way of any other claimant for exclusive honors. Thus, a fact that would be taken for granted in any other society—that the war had been won by the achievements and sacrifices of the people—in Soviet conditions became loaded with political implications. As Soviet postwar propaganda showed, the record of the people's role in the war had to give way to the political megalomania of the regime—not that the people's contribution was ever openly contested; it was simply displaced.

It will not be necessary to show in any detail how the people's role was evaluated during the war, since everything that could be said in this regard was said by Stalin in one dramatic speech at the war's end. This is what he publicly declared in his victory toast to the Russian people:

Our Government made not a few errors. We experienced at moments a desperate situation in 1941–42, when our Army was retreating, abandoning our own villages and towns of the Ukraine, Belorussia, Moldavia, the Leningrad region, the Baltic area, and the Karelo-Finnish Republic, abandoning them because there was no other way out. A different people could have said to our Government: "You have failed to justify our expectations. Go away. We shall install another government, which will conclude peace with Germany and assure us a quiet life." The Russian people, however, did not take this path because it trusted the correctness of the policy of its Government, and it made sacrifices to ensure the rout of Germany. This confidence of the Russian people in the Soviet Government proved to be that decisive force that ensured the historic victory over the enemy of humanity—over fascism.[35]

With such a testimonial from such an authority, the Russian people could face the postwar period with confidence that their role in history was assured.

THE ROLE OF THE ALLIES

The response of the Western Allies to Russia's plight in 1941 was prompt and generous, and the material and military contribution the West made to the final victory was very great. Allied material aid was extended at a time and under conditions that imposed a very real sacrifice on the Allies' own war effort. In addition, as the war progressed, the Allies brought to bear a military pressure on Germany that contributed materially to speeding the collapse of the German war machine.

According to American sources, the value of American Lend-Lease shipments to Russia during the war totaled over $11 billion. British shipments and American private relief added considerably to this total. Walter Kerr, in his book *The Russian Army,* presents additional figures that bring out in a more graphic way the actual significance of this aid to the Soviet Army. During the first year of deliveries alone, he says, Washington and London shipped to Russia 3,052 planes, 4,084 tanks, 30,031 vehicles, and 831,000 tons of miscellaneous supplies, of which the major part got through. As Kerr points out, the relative value of these figures can be grasped if they are compared with the 1,136 planes and 2,001 tanks, which, according to Russian claims, the Germans lost during 52 days of the heaviest fighting in the first year of the war.[36] There are many indications from Russian sources, too, of the value the Soviet Union placed on this aid during the war. Stalin's petulance at delays in the arrival of American equipment indicates this. The impress that Allied aid made on the Soviet population, indications of which are scattered throughout Soviet literature, is another sign of its scope and significance. Even the language has recorded the dimensions of American wartime aid, in its transformation of the name "Willys" into a Russian household word.

The composition of American material aid was geared to Soviet needs. Fighting equipment comprised a significant percentage of the whole. If Stalin's figures on the Soviet annual wartime production of aircraft are to be believed, American-supplied aircraft approached something like one-tenth of Soviet wartime production. But as Soviet industry began to produce more military items, greater emphasis was placed on nonmilitary goods, such as machine tools, industrial plants, and raw materials. General Deane, the head of the United States Military Mission charged with coordinating the Lend-Lease program, listed trucks, petroleum products, food, and railroad equipment—in that order—as being the most important items sent to the U.S.S.R. Regarding the role of American trucks in the Soviet Army's operations, he said:

When I made a trip to the Russian front in July, 1944, we encountered American trucks everywhere. They appeared to be the only sort of vehicles used for convoy work. The roads were jammed with transportation of all descriptions, but except for American trucks there did not appear to be enough of any one kind to set up convoys which could be moved as units.[37]

As for the Allied military role in the war, the story is familiar enough to need no retelling here. Beginning in Africa, in 1942, the Allies began to build up a steadily mounting pressure on Germany that engaged and wasted the dwindling resources so desperately needed on the Eastern front. Soviet propaganda made much of the claim later that no German units were withdrawn from the Eastern front as a result of Allied operations (in fact, however, at least two SS divisions were withdrawn to meet the Normandy invasion),[38] but this is beside the point. The real contribution of the Allies was measured not in the juggling of German divisions that it produced, but in the cost in German energies that a series of Allied second fronts—in Africa, Sicily, Italy, and France—absorbed.

In considering how the Soviet Union interpreted the Allied role in the war in its postwar propaganda, and how this interpretation compared with the picture it presented to its people during the war itself, it will be best to take up separately the major charges and distortions introduced into the postwar accounts.

The Charge of Allied Responsibility for the Outbreak of the War

Soviet postwar propaganda was not content merely to minimize the Allied role in the war, but sought actively to transform the image of the Allies from partners in the anti-Hitler coalition into crypto-enemies of the Soviet Union and virtual allies of Hitler. The principal device used to achieve this end was to hammer home the accusation that the real aim of Western policy before the war had been to isolate the U.S.S.R. and, in the final account, to embroil it in war with Germany.

In its broadest application, this charge affected the official Soviet interpretation of the whole prewar period. Beginning with the

Paris Peace Conference, at which it was asserted that the "Russian question" occupied the primary place,[39] almost every major event of European diplomacy affecting the U.S.S.R. was made to fit into this interpretative framework. The Dawes Plan, which loosed a "golden rain of American dollars" on German war industry; the Four Power Pact, which signified Anglo-French willingness to come to terms with fascism; the Polish-German nonaggression pact of 1934, which set a precedent for replacing the principle of collective security by a system of bilateral pacts; the Anglo-German naval agreement of 1935, which proclaimed Britain's disavowal of the principle of restricting German remilitarization—all were seen in the Soviet account as stages in the consistent Western policy of isolating the U.S.S.R. and encouraging German aggression.[40]

The major event affected by this line of interpretation was, of course, the Munich agreement. The facts surrounding this episode were such as to lend themselves to almost any indictment of the strategy and morality of Western policy that the Soviet Union would wish to make. The agreement was, in fact, strategically defective in that it excluded the Soviet Union from the joint action of the directing nations and morally defective in that it legalized violence. But these indictments, recognized as valid in Western literature, were not broad enough for the purposes of Soviet postwar propaganda. Instead, Stalin's phrase of 1939, that the Munich agreement was "the price of an undertaking [by Germany] to launch war on the Soviet Union," was resurrected as the basis of the Soviet historical interpretation.* The Western leaders were

* The quotation is from Stalin's report to the Eighteenth Party Congress and is given in the sense attributed to it by the 1948 Sovinform pamphlet *Falsificators of History*. It was in this sense that it was always quoted by Soviet authors thereafter. Actually, in the original, Stalin had been less categorical and had given the phrase an ironical twist. This is what he said: "One might think that the districts of Czechoslovakia were yielded to Germany as the price of an undertaking to launch war on the Soviet Union." Cf. *The Land of Socialism Today and Tomorrow* (Moscow, 1939), p. 16. Postwar writers seldom attempted to bolster this declamatory assessment of the Munich agreement with argument or facts. The most industrious

portrayed as active plotters with Hitler for war. In Soviet postwar historiography, the word "deal" (*sgovor*) became the official cachet of Munich, and historians who had seen in the Western behavior at Munich a "concession" or "capitulation" to Nazi threats were made to see their error.

It will be seen that the crux of the Soviet interpretation was this hostile appraisal of the motivations of Western conduct. By this token, the account of Western prewar diplomacy given out by the Soviet Union during the war was somewhat more balanced. It was set forth in its most complete and authoritative form in the semi-official *History of Diplomacy,* the final volume of which was published in 1945.[41] This book, it should be stressed, gave an ideological interpretation of Western diplomacy that was, in its general terms, every bit as hostile as any offered in the postwar historiography. In its introduction, it directly accused the West of having sought to direct Hitler's aggression against the Soviet Union. It was laced with ideological dicta that placed Western motives and behavior in a discreditable light. Yet it contained features that probably would not have been in it had the book been written several years later.

A particularly notable feature, in this regard, was the favorable treatment given to those British leaders, such as Churchill, Eden, Duff Cooper, Lloyd George, and others, who opposed the policy of Chamberlain. Their utterances were quoted approvingly, Churchill's at considerable length, and, whatever the intentions of

effort to put documentary flesh on the bare bones of Stalin's intuition was made by B. Shteyn in *Voprosy Istorii,* No. 2 (1951). In a critical analysis of volumes I and II, 3rd series, of the *Documents on British Foreign Policy, 1919–1939,* Shteyn offered a tortured exegesis of the records of the Munich meeting and of the meeting between Hitler and Chamberlain on the following day, to show: (1) that the British representatives, at the time, looked upon the agreement as an implicit bargain, calling for some *quid pro quo* on the part of Germany, and (2) that Hitler was given to understand that the U.S.S.R. lay outside the sphere of British interests. The deal was completed, according to this interpretation, by the Anglo-German and Franco-German agreements for mutual consultation, which constituted, in effect, a system of Western nonaggression pacts.

the authors, the impression was created that British policy awaited only the arrival of such men at the helm to turn to an honorable course. Secondly, the book was less categorical than the later official historiography regarding the alleged deliberate aim of the Western leaders to turn Hitler against the Soviet Union. It did contain such sentences as this: "The compliancy of Anglo-French diplomacy encouraged Hitlerite Germany to further realization of its aggressive plans. Among the participants of the Munich conference there was obvious understanding as to the direction of the German attack."[42] But this was a cut below the charge that Munich was the "price of an undertaking," and besides, the whole spirit of the narrative stressed the weakness of the West rather than its duplicity. Chamberlain was repeatedly referred to as "aging," as being "seventy years of age," and the Western behavior at Munich was specifically described as a capitulation, a designation that even appeared in a chapter title.[43] This impression of Western weakness was further underlined by a special chapter at the end dealing with the methods of "bourgeois diplomacy," in which the tactics of terrorization used by Hitler against the Western leaders were described. Finally, a stylistic feature that distinguished this book from later publications was the ample references to Western sources that it offered, both in footnotes and in a formal bibliography. In sum, therefore, the picture of Western prewar diplomacy that the Soviet Union offered at the end of the war was, although deprecatory of the West, not devoid of some appreciation of the human weaknesses that conditioned it.

The Deprecation of Allied Material Aid

For Soviet postwar propaganda, any acknowledgment of the magnitude and usefulness of Allied aid could serve no political purpose. It would document the indebtedness of the Soviet Union to a foreign state, which the Soviet Union would be loath to admit in any event, least of all to the "bulwark of world capitalism." Moreover, it would diminish to some degree the luster of the

Soviet Union's own industrial achievements, which were claimed to rest on the farsighted industrialization programs carried out by the regime during the Five-Year plans. Thus, the matter of Allied supplies was mentioned very sparingly in Soviet postwar accounts of the war and, where mentioned, was always presented as an exchange for Soviet raw materials or as a paltry recompense for the Russian contributions of blood and time.

This picture represented a considerable departure from the record that the Soviet Government permitted its people to see during the war itself. Soviet wartime reporting of Allied material aid was undoubtedly, as Professor Barghoorn points out in his book *The Soviet Image of the United States,* inadequate and ungenerous, but it was, by his own evidence, a far cry from the treatment given this subject in postwar historiography. Official conferences dealing with American-British supplies were given ceremonial publicity, and each anniversary of the signing of the Lend-Lease agreement was observed in the Soviet press. Moreover, American official releases regarding Lend-Lease shipments were published in the Soviet press "in whole or in part," according to Barghoorn. Finally, Soviet Government officials made statements from time to time acknowledging the significance of this aid. Stalin in his May Day speech of 1942, for example, assigned first place among the freedom-loving countries to Great Britain and the U.S., "with whom we are bound by ties of friendship, and who render our country more and more military aid against the German fascist invaders." Again, in 1945, in a statement to President Truman, Stalin said that American Lend-Lease shipments had "played an important role and to a substantial degree assisted the successful completion" of the war.[44] When it is recalled that this coverage was accompanied by frequent press references to the industrial and military power of the Allies, it must be concluded that the Soviet people arrived at the end of the war with some impression, however inadequate, of the material contribution the Allies had made to the victory.

The Second-Front Issue

The most publicized of the issues affecting the Allied role in the war was the question of the "second front," and on this question the difference between Soviet wartime and postwar attitudes was less distinct than on the other questions considered here. The basis of the Soviet postwar charge that the Allies had shown bad faith in this matter was the joint communiqué published in London and Washington after the Molotov visit in the spring of 1942. The communiqué said in part that "in the course of the conversations, full understanding was reached with regard to the urgent task of creating a second front in Europe in 1942."[45] Churchill has explained that the purpose of the communiqué was to make the Germans apprehensive and hold as many of their troops in the west as possible. So as not to mislead the Russians, he took care to give Molotov an *aide-mémoire,* stating that he could "give no promise in the matter."[46] In postwar comment on the subject, Soviet propaganda ignored the *aide-mémoire.* Instead, it bent every effort to show that the Allies had gone back on their word and had done so, moreover, with the deliberate aim of dragging out the war and exhausting the Russians.

The Soviet people were given a somewhat milder foretaste of this interpretation in Soviet propaganda treatment of this subject during the war. Stalin, for example, used the absence of a second front in 1941 as an explanation for the failure of the Russian Army to hold the German invasion, and the same excuse was put forward on a much broader propaganda scale in 1942, being presented in a particularly bitter manner toward the end of the year, during the siege of Stalingrad. Some of the bitterness began to go out of the issue after the Allied North African invasion, but it remained as an undercurrent of accusation in Soviet comments both on the course of the war and on Allied contributions to it.

The Disparagement of the Normandy Invasion

Soviet postwar propaganda interpreted the Normandy invasion in such a way as to place Allied political motives and military capabilities in the worst possible light. It was stated that the Allies undertook the Normandy invasion only to forestall the inevitable singlehanded triumph of the Soviet Union. Moreover, it was charged that the Allies deliberately delayed their breakout from the Normandy beachhead for two and a half months, meanwhile watching developments on the Soviet-German front and playing with the possibilities of a compromise peace. In all of this, Soviet postwar propaganda placed great stress on the alleged inconsequential resistance put up by the Germans to the Allied invasion. It was claimed that the German divisions in Europe were not of first combat quality. During the whole period of the Normandy invasion, according to Soviet postwar propaganda, not a single German division was transferred from the Soviet front. Consequently, no significance could be attached to the Normandy invasion as easing the situation in any substantial degree on the Eastern front.

A highly derogatory appraisal of Allied military capabilities was also given in connection with the Ardennes battle and the final advance through Germany. The former was presented as a major collapse of the Allied military position, which would have been fatal had not Stalin, in response to Churchill's urgent plea, advanced the date of the Soviet winter offensive and thus forced the Germans to abandon their attack and withdraw their forces to the Eastern front. The final Allied advance through Germany was also explained as the result of the German political decision to concentrate all forces against the Russians and to leave the way open for the Allies to reach Berlin first.

This interpretation was quite different from the account of Allied military operations given to the Soviet people during the war. Again, on this point, Professor Barghoorn emphasizes the niggardliness of the Soviet coverage compared with standards normally expected from allies. He stresses, for example, the fact that Allied operations were often ignored in Soviet editorial comment on the war, and that after the first year of the war, news of Allied activities no longer appeared on the front page of Soviet newspapers.[47] Barghoorn is undoubtedly correct in seeing in the Soviet press treatment of the Allied part in the war a reflection of that suspicious and reserved attitude toward the Allies that many wartime observers have documented. At the same time, it must be recognized that the Russians shared with the other participants in the war the natural tendency to view the operations of their own forces in greatly enlarged perspective. Thus, if the Americans could have their Midway, and the British their El Alamein, the Russians could with equal merit have their Stalingrad and Kursk. In this matter of viewing the war from the standpoint of their own triumphs and tragedies, the Russians were not alone.

Despite the distortion resulting from this as well as from the ever-present ideological considerations, the Soviet people during the war were given a much more accurate picture of Allied military operations than at any time later. The effect was undoubtedly strong in that the most generous accounts of Allied operations were given during the latter stages of the war, so that the Soviet people must have arrived at the day of victory with a fairly strong feeling of respect for the contributions the Allies had made to the joint cause. The most glowing appraisal of Allied achievements was made by Stalin himself at the time of the Normandy invasion, and it would be difficult to conceive of a more unstinting expression of praise than he gave on that occasion: "One cannot but acknowledge that the history of war knows no other similar undertaking as regards breadth of design, vastness of scale, and high skill of execution. . . . History will record this deed as an achievement of the highest order."[48]

In summing up, it may be said that the Soviet Union showed a perceptibly more friendly, or at least a less hostile, attitude toward the Allies during the war than after it. With respect to at least two

of the issues we have considered—Allied material aid and the
Normandy invasion—the Soviet Union entered the postwar period
with a public record that was recognizably related to the facts and
calculated to convey a generally respectful impression of the Allied role in the war. It may be added that this impression was undoubtedly strengthened by other facts concerning the Soviet wartime attitude toward the Allies that were not considered above:
the emphasis on the "coalition" character of the war, the friendly
interpretations of Western personalities and societies, the glimpses
of Western culture that were permitted, etc. As Barghoorn points
out, the relaxation of Soviet ideological controls associated with
these facts had resulted, by war's end, in implanting in a "considerable section of Soviet opinion" the conviction that the wartime
collaboration between Russia and the Anglo-Americans should be
not merely continued after the war but immensely strengthened.[49]

THE PACIFIC WAR

At the end of the war in Europe, the Soviet Union at last began
to move toward participation in the war against Japan. During the
preceding four years, it had followed a very cautious policy toward
Japan, carefully avoiding, particularly during the earlier part of the
war, any statement or act that might provoke Japanese retaliation.
Formally, its relations with Japan were based on the neutrality
treaty of April, 1941, which, like the nonaggression pact with
Germany in 1939, had given the Soviet Union a measure of security while deflecting aggression toward the Western states. Immediately after Pearl Harbor, the United States broached the
question of Soviet participation in the Pacific war with the Soviet
Government, returning to this issue intermittently in a variety of
contexts during the following years, but the Soviet Union parried
all such overtures. Even after the Yalta agreement, which provided
for Soviet entry within three months after the end of the war with
Germany and assured the Soviet Union of tangible profits from

this enterprise, the Soviet Union seemed reluctant to commit itself
to action. In the two meetings that the United States planning
group in Moscow was able to arrange with Soviet representatives
in the months after Yalta, discussions never got beyond organizational matters. Moreover, the survey parties for Kamchatka and
the Amur River area, which had been authorized at Yalta as part
of the planning for future joint operations, never entered Soviet
territory.[50]

Shortly after the end of the war in Europe, however, the Soviet
Government began to show a more active interest in the Pacific
war. This enhanced interest coincided with the beginning of a
series of overtures from the Japanese that indicated to the Soviet
Government that Japan was angling for a way out of the war.
These overtures at first centered on a Japanese proposal for a new
basis of understanding to take the place of the neutrality treaty
that the Soviet Union had denounced in 1945.[51] In July, before and
during the Potsdam conference, Japanese efforts to engage Soviet
mediation of a compromise peace became more pointed. On July
13, Ambassador Sato approached the Soviet Foreign Ministry with
a request for Soviet good offices in arranging peace, and a week
later (during the conference), asked the Soviet Government to re-
ceive a special emissary from Tokyo to discuss the matter in detail.[52] Stalin informed President Truman of these approaches at
Potsdam, and, for the first time, Soviet military authorities began
to adopt a more purposeful attitude in their planning discussions
with the Allies.[53] The Allies were promised that the Soviet Union
would enter the Pacific war late in August, the exact date to be
contingent on the satisfactory conclusion of negotiations with
China.[54]

On August 6, the first atomic bomb was dropped on Hiroshima.
On August 8, Molotov summoned the Japanese Ambassador to in-
form him that the Soviet Union would consider itself in a state of
war with Japan as of the following day. On August 14, the Soviet

negotiations with China, which had been mentioned at Potsdam as a condition of Soviet entry into the war, were concluded.

The Soviet invasion of Manchuria by three army groups under the over-all command of Marshal Vasilevskiy began on August 9. Faced by a demoralized and poorly armed adversary, the Soviet invasion forces made very rapid progress, even during the first six days of the invasion, when Japan was still officially at war. On August 14, Japan announced its surrender, but the Soviet Union refused to accept it. Two days later, the Soviet Far Eastern Command announced that the Emperor's capitulation was unsatisfactory, since it did not contain specific instructions to the troops to lay down their arms and that, consequently, offensive operations would continue. Even the direct capitulation of the Command of the Kwantung Army, on August 19, failed to halt the rush of the Soviet troops,[55] and official surrender was recognized by the Soviet Government only on September 2, the date of the formal ceremonies in Tokyo Bay.

The Japanese collapse was the result of the cumulative punishment Japan had received in the course of its unequal struggle with the United States and the exhaustion of its strength in China. Neither the atomic bomb nor the Russian declaration of war was decisive in this outcome. The crucial decision to capitulate was taken in the night of August 9–10, when the intervention of the Emperor was invoked to break the irresolution in the Japanese Supreme War-Directing Council. In his statement to the Council announcing his decision to accept surrender, the Emperor mentioned neither the atomic bomb nor the Soviet invasion. The Western historical record overwhelmingly supports the conclusion that Japan was hopelessly defeated long before the decision to accept surrender took place. As the *United States Strategic Bombing Survey* concludes: "Certainly prior to 31st December, 1945, and in all probability prior to 1st November, 1945, Japan would have surrendered even if the atomic bomb had not been dropped, even if

Russia had not entered the war, and even if no invasion had been planned or contemplated."[56]

Which factor, however—the atomic bomb or the Soviet attack—actually triggered the Japanese decision to announce surrender on August 14? A conclusive answer probably cannot be given. Todshikazu Kase, who, as an official in the Japanese Foreign Ministry, was in a position to know the influences that shaped Japanese policy at that time, sums up the question thus:

Was it the atomic bomb or Russian participation in the war that was responsible for the surrender? That is a difficult question to answer. It will probably always remain a debatable point. But to us who knew the inner development it seems that neither of the two basically changed the course of the war. It is certain that we would have surrendered in due time even without the terrific chastisement of the bomb or the terrible shock of the Russian attack. However, it cannot also be denied that both the bomb and the Russians facilitated our surrender.[57]

The principal issue raised by the Soviet account of the Pacific war was the interpretation of the Japanese surrender. The Soviet Union from the beginning maintained that it was the Soviet declaration of war and the defeat of the Kwantung Army, rather than the atomic bomb, that forced the Japanese to capitulate. The Soviet argument was based principally on three assertions: (1) that the Allies had achieved no significant military successes against the Japanese during the course of the Pacific war; (2) that, in Manchuria, the main military strength of Japan remained throughout the war untouched;* and (3) that, in 1945, Japan was still capable of continuing the war for another two years at least. This last assertion was based on American military estimates, made in

* A rare admission by a Soviet source that the Japanese Manchurian garrison had been reduced during the war was made in the *New Times*, August 15, 1945, p. 12: "Only in the latter half of 1943 and in 1944, when it became perfectly evident to the Japanese militarists that the plans of the Nazi command had failed, did the Japanese General Staff begin somewhat to reduce the number of troops concentrated for an attack on the Soviet Union."

1944 and 1945, of the requirements for the invasion of the Japanese home islands.

The role of the atomic bomb was usually ignored or summarily dismissed in Soviet accounts of the Japanese surrender. The most circumstantial Soviet argument on this point was offered by V. Avarin in his second book on the Pacific war.[58] It was based on the data presented in the *United States Strategic Bombing Survey* regarding the deliberations in the Japanese Government during the last days before the decision to surrender was taken. Part of Avarin's argument was based on the timing of these events. The atomic bomb, he observed, was dropped on August 6, and resulted in no particular reaction in Japanese official circles. The Soviet declaration of war reached Tokyo on the morning of August 9, and was followed by a frantic series of official meetings, concluding with the Imperial Conference in the night of August 9–10. Part of his argument was based also on the substance of the discussions. The key element here was the statement of the Emperor announcing his decision to accept surrender. In it, he did not mention the atomic bomb, but said in part (according to Avarin's translation): "To continue the war in the international situation that has arisen, and given the situation within Japan, would mean the destruction of the whole nation."* This, according to Avarin, proved that the point at issue was "not the atomic bomb or strategic bombing, but 'the international situation which had arisen,' i.e., the entrance of the Soviet Union into the war against Japan."

Unlike many of the other issues discussed in this chapter, there was very little development or change in the Soviet interpretation of the Japanese surrender during the postwar period. According to Max Beloff, in his book *Soviet Policy in the Far East, 1944–1951*, the attribution of the Japanese collapse exclusively to Soviet

* The Emperor's words, as given in the *Strategic Bombing Survey*, p. 8, are as follows: "Thinking about the world situation and the internal Japanese situation, to continue the war means nothing but the destruction of the whole nation." Avarin obviously shaded his translation to support his argument.

victories in Manchuria remained a constant of Soviet comment on
this subject from the end of the war on.[59] All the major elements
of the Soviet account that have been described above were present
in the earliest noted analyses of this event. Colonel M. Tolchenov,
a prominent military writer, set out the main lines of this argument
in 1945, although in somewhat less categorical terms than later
became customary. He cited Allied military estimates as proof that
Japan was still capable of resistance at the end and claimed that
most foreign newspapers recognized that Soviet intervention was
"one of the decisive factors" compelling the enemy to lay down
his arms.[60] An accompanying article assessed the significance of
the atomic bomb, expressing some cautious optimism as to its
future peacetime implications, but concluding that it was irrelevant
to the final outcome of the Pacific war and invoking the authority
of General Arnold and General Chennault in support of this conclusion.[61]

In summing up this inquiry into the major issues raised by the
Soviet historiography of the war, it may be observed that all were
products of the incompatibility between the regime's wartime
record and its postwar policies. The critical issues were those that
touched one or another of the two basic embarrassing facts of the
war: the mistakes and sufferings of the early period, and the wartime friendship with the capitalist states. As for the Soviet Union's
public record on these issues as the postwar period opened, the picture was mixed and undefined. Soviet statements and propaganda
during the war provided a platform for any of several possible lines
of Soviet policy development and certainly for a more liberal
course than Soviet policy actually took.

2

The Development of the
Postwar Official Line

The development of the Soviet official line on the war paralleled and reflected the pace and direction of general postwar policies. By 1946, at least, the basic decisions affecting these policies had been taken, and whatever uncertainties and vacillations about particular questions might remain, the Kremlin thereafter followed along the lines of these decisions. Cooperation with the West was rejected in favor of pushing as fast and as far as possible to exploit and consolidate territorial gains in eastern Europe; encouragement of individual initiative within the Soviet Union was replaced by the full stringency of dictatorship. The Soviet leaders turned their faces against the dawn of a peaceful life in the world, and with remarkable abruptness the complex organism of the Soviet Union was wrenched into conformity with the leaders' wishes.

To put the machinery of ideological mobilization, which this policy entailed, into operation, the leadership applied a technique that may be called criticism by analogy. Shocks were administered to key areas of Soviet activity with the aim of stimulating favorable responses throughout the social organism. One Soviet writer later described the effect these methods had within one field of activity, that of literary criticism. "Criticism worked out its theses," he said, "not through constant, thoughtful observations and syntheses, but

38 THE SOVIET HISTORY OF WORLD WAR II

incident by incident, as this or that writer fell into error, and the Party press criticized him."[1] A series of highly publicized "cases"—the condemnation of the journals *Leningrad* and *Zvezda,* the discussion of Aleksandrov's textbook, the decree on music, the criticism of Varga, the biology controversy—extended direct Party influence into all the major fields of Soviet intellectual life. These cases imparted a charged, dramatic quality to the postwar ideological climate and added rich overtones of meaning to the propaganda texts that were concurrently pouring from the Party presses.

An understanding of this paratextual quality of the Soviet postwar ideological climate is particularly important for the study of the development of the historiography of the war. A striking paradox of the Soviet postwar reinterpretation of the war is that it was effected without a propaganda campaign, in the usual sense of the word, and without a history text.* The regular newspaper articles on the subject, by their characteristic sparseness and rigidity, convey only a faint idea of the psychological background that was being created concurrently by parallel lines of propaganda. The Soviet propaganda assault on the West, for example, had become the dominant theme of the Soviet press well before it found literal

* Stalin's wartime writings and speeches collected in *The Great Patriotic War of the Soviet Union,* the fifth and last edition of which was published in 1949, constituted for all practical purposes the only official history of the war during his lifetime. Other book-length treatments were popularizations drawn from this source and the other propaganda sources described in this chapter. The most substantial of these were: the article on the war in the special "SSSR" volume of the *Bolshaya Sovetskaya Entsyklopedia* (1947); I. I. Mints, I. M. Razgon, A. L. Sidorov, *Der Grosse Vaterländische Krieg der Sowjetunion* (Berlin, 1947), published separately only in German; A. Krutikov, *Velikaya otechestvennaya voyna sovetskogo soyuza: popularnyy ocherk* (Moscow, 1947); I. V. Anisimov, G. V. Kuzmin, *Velikaya otechestvennaya voyna sovetskogo soyuza 1941–1945 gg.* (Moscow, 1952); S. Golikov, *Vydayushchiyesya pobedy sovetskoy armii v velikoy otechestvennoy voyne* (Moscow, 1952, 1954); E. Burdzhalov, *Velikaya otechestvennaya voyna sovetskogo soyuza, 1941–1945 gg.* (Moscow, 1953); F. D. Vorob'yev, V. M. Kravtsov, *Pobedy sovetskikh vooruzhennykh sil v velikoy otechestvennoy voyne 1941–1945 gg.* (Moscow, 1953, 1954). A useful bibliography of this whole subject is contained in *Voprosy Istorii,* No. 6 (1961), pp. 115–25.

expression in the historical treatments of the war. By the second half of 1947, this motif had virtually eradicated other themes from the Soviet press, and anti-Western propaganda had become so vicious that Ambassador Smith was moved to lodge a formal protest with the Soviet Government.[2] To understand the atmosphere that was created around the history of the war, therefore, it is necessary to consider not only the texts specifically devoted to this subject but the whole complex of actions by which the Party drove home the key elements of the interpretation it wished to impress. The present chapter will consider both the direct and indirect mechanisms of Party influence on public thinking about the war.

THE MAIN PROPAGANDA LINE

In the postwar period, the prodigies of sustained exclamation that had characterized much of the wartime writing about the war rapidly gave way to highly stylized recitations of formulas derived from official utterances. The first and major source of these formulas was Stalin's speech of February 9, 1946, delivered to the electors of the Stalin district of Moscow. As subsequent propaganda showed, this was the take-off point for the postwar official reinterpretation of the war.

Stalin's speech was, in effect, a manifesto of the Party's resurgence into the center of Soviet life. Calling the war "a kind of examination for the Soviet system," Stalin summed up the results of that test. In substance it came to this: The war had been won not primarily because of the valor of the troops or the sacrifices of the people, but because of the soundness of Party policies and the strength of the system that these policies had created. The basic ingredients of victory, Stalin asserted, were the sinews of economic strength that the Party, foreseeing the advent of war, had wisely created in the prewar years. "It would be a mistake to think," said Stalin, "that such a historic victory could have been won if the whole country had not [been] prepared beforehand for active defense. . . . It would be a still greater mistake to say that we won only owing to the gallantry of our troops."[3]

This gist of Stalin's remarks highlights the basic elements of what was to become the official propaganda interpretation of the war over the next few years. The most striking feature of the account, in comparison with those of a year or two before, was the shift of emphasis it achieved from the military events of the war to the underlying political and economic factors that were said to have conditioned them. This had two immediate effects, which remained characteristic of the postwar accounts. It enlarged the role of the Party in the war as the agent of these political and economic factors and diminished the role of the people, the soldiers, and the military leaders. Stalin's contraposing of gallantry to economic realities as factors of victory, which was essentially deprecatory of the former, symbolized a trend toward a more abstract and bloodless portrayal of the war that became more pronounced as time went on.

The first major occasion for press commentary on the war was the celebration of Armed Forces Day in 1946, which occurred a few days after Stalin's speech. The general outlines of Stalin's analysis were clearly apparent in the editorial observances. So that there could be no mistake in the emphasis desired, *Pravda* italicized the key points: "Our Soviet *social* system conquered. Our Soviet *state* system conquered. Our *armed forces* conquered."[4] On Victory Day, a few months later, this same line of interpretation was elaborated. "The Soviet people know that the great victory won by our Motherland in the cruelest of wars that the history of mankind has ever known was above all a victory of our social and state system; it was the result of the wise and far-seeing Stalinist policy of the Bolshevik Party, which prepared the country for active defense and created the powerful Red Army."[5] Apart from the content of these articles, the general character of the press treatment of the major war anniversaries reinforced the political nature of the interpretation that Stalin had given. It has already been mentioned that Zhukov's name did not appear in the press observance of the first anniversary of Victory Day. No other military figure was named in *Pravda* on that day either, nor on the other major anniversaries of the next few years. In addition, the celebration was subdued, almost perfunctory. The anniversary of the invasion, June 22, was observed with a small editorial in *Pravda* that was all but overshadowed by the concurrent discussion of the new Five-Year Plan for the R.S.F.S.R.

Despite this display of propaganda regimentation, there were features of the first postwar year's commentary on the war that showed that all details of the official interpretation had not yet been worked out. *Pravda,* in its Victory Day editorial, for example, evoked a faint memory of the mood of the wartime period by recalling Stalin's salute of the year before to his "fellow countrymen and fellow countrywomen." It mentioned also the soldiers who that day were honored for their part in raising the flag over the Reichstag.[6] The historian Mints, in an article in *Pravda* on the same day, gave a more generous appraisal of the people's part in the war. He also praised the Soviet military leaders: "The Soviet people raised from their ranks the glorious commanders who comprise the pleiad of Stalinist marshals."[7] The military writer Zamyatin, on June 22, also succeeded in recalling something of the military leaders' contribution to the victory. He spoke of the "genius leadership" of Stalin, but treated it in a general way and attributed the planning of the war to the more impersonal "Stavka." He also emphasized the ability of "our generals and officers" to effect complex maneuvers.[8] These variations from the central political and economic theses indicated that the treatment of the war in official propaganda had not yet been fully formularized.

The year 1947 marked a long step toward complete standardization and also added an important new element to the official formula. *Pravda* writers showed particular reserve and caution on the war during 1947, and the use of direct quotations from Stalin increased. Also, the amount of space devoted to the war anniversaries was still further reduced, and war themes were often subordinated to current political commentary. The shift in style is clearly revealed by a comparison of Galaktionov's Armed Forces Day article of 1947, which was a turgid gloss on Stalin's electoral speech, with his highly colored, exclamatory article of the year before. The *Pravda* editorials of May 9 and June 22 interspersed current political propaganda with the war observances and in part used the latter as springboards for homilies on Soviet foreign policy or the Five-Year Plan.

The new element in the official interpretation of the war was the doctrine of the counteroffensive. It was thrust into Soviet propaganda by Stalin's letter to Colonel Razin, which was published in February, 1947. The essential point of the letter, insofar as it touched the history of the war, was Stalin's implied claim that he had applied a highly subtle and complex strategy, the "counteroffensive." Because of the importance of this doctrine in the Soviet interpretation of the war, it will be treated separately later. Here it will be sufficient to note the intrusion of this doctrine, in 1947, into the regular propaganda texts on the war.

The first major treatment of the doctrine in *Pravda,* mentioned briefly previously, appears to have been Talenskiy's article "Bankruptcy of the Plans of the Aggressors," published on June 22. After mentioning Stalin's letter to Razin, and Stalin's praise of Kutuzov as one of the early exponents of the counteroffensive, Talenskiy went on to say that this strategy had been brought to perfection only in World War II.

This form of struggle achieved its greatest development in terms of scale, scientific depth, purposefulness, and results in the command activities of Comrade Stalin. . . . In the subsequent course of the war [after the battle of Moscow] the counteroffensive was applied with unvarying success in the battles of Stalingrad and Kursk. The counteroffensive in Stalinist strategy was that form of struggle which, in the military aspect, turned the course of the war to our advantage.

Since the doctrine of the "counteroffensive" to some extent came to overshadow the doctrine of "active defense," it will be appropriate to pause here for a moment to consider how the latter doctrine had developed to this point. In its original meaning—which it generally carried during the war itself, particularly in the writings of military authors—it expressed a military idea. It derived from Stalin's Order of the Day, No. 308, of September 18, 1941. In it, Stalin praised the guards units for their "active defense, combined with counterattacks." He gave the concept the sense of a transitional strategy by speaking of its morale uses, of the goal of a subsequent transition to the offensive inherent in it.

They did not wait for the adversary to strike them and push them back, but themselves went over to counterattacks, in order to feel out the weak places of the adversary, to improve their positions, and, at the same time, to temper their regiments in the process of counterattacks to prepare them for an offensive.[9]

Somewhat later, the concept began to take on a political meaning. In this sense, it expressed the idea that the actions of the Soviet Army in defense were preplanned to hold back the progress of the enemy until the permanently operating factors of war could be brought into play. Stalin's Order of the Day of February 23, 1942, which defined the formula of the permanently operating factors, as well as his May Day speech of 1942, contributed to this meaning.[10] The more direct source of the postwar flourishing of the concept was Stalin's electoral speech mentioned earlier. The emphasis in that speech on the economic factors of victory reinforced the idea that the early retreats were simply means to an end, a device that provided time for the decisive factors to come into operation. Several examples from the materials we have been reviewing will show how this concept was used during the early postwar period. Zamyatin, in his article of June 22, 1946, said: "In these conditions, an extraordinarily responsible and heavy task was posed for the Soviet Supreme Command, for the Red Army—

by means of an active strategic defense, to hold back the advance of the hostile armies into the depths of the Soviet territory, and to win time for the necessary reorganization of the whole economy of the country directly to war requirements, and for mobilizing and deploying the main forces of the Red Army."[11] Colonel General N. Chibisov, in an article on Victory Day, 1947, wrote: "1941 and 1942 entered into history as the years of active defense, which exhausted the forces of the enemy and brought to naught all his original advantages."[12] The *Pravda* editorial on the second anniversary of the invasion said: "The wise and far-seeing Stalinist policy of industrializing the country and collectivizing agriculture created the material possibilities necessary for the active defense of our country."[13]

We can resume the review of the main line of Soviet propaganda on the war by noting that the year 1948 marked the virtual completion of this development. Armed Forces Day of 1948, the thirtieth anniversary of the Red Army, was observed by a celebration in the Bolshoi Theater and an important speech by Minister of the Armed Forces Bulganin. This speech provided a new synthesis of the interpretations that had grown out of Stalin's electoral speech and gave fresh impetus to the trends that they represented. By emphasizing a distinction between military science, which, it was made clear, was the province of Stalin, and military art, which was the province of lesser commanders, it wove together the doctrine of the pre-eminent significance of political and economic factors in war with the burgeoning cult of Stalin's military genius. "Military art," said Bulganin, "is a constituent part of military science, embracing tactics, operational art, and strategy; i.e., it has to do with the study of questions relating to the methods of conducting military operations and wars as a whole. Military science, in addition to questions of military art, takes up the questions of the economic and moral potentialities of countries."[14] This doctrine, which provided a sophisticated framework for all the claims that had been put forward regarding Stalin's leadership in the war, remained an important element of the Soviet official interpretation of the war.

In all respects, Bulganin's speech, and the attendant anniversary articles, represented the full blossoming of the official version of World War II. The eclipse of the military leaders by the shadow of Stalin, all the more striking because of the nature of the occasion, was virtually complete. Some of the marshals—Vasilevskiy, Govorov, Konev, Meretskov, et al—appeared on the stage of the Bolshoi Theater with the leaders, but none of them was named in the articles in *Pravda,* and Zhukov was nowhere in evidence.

The denigration of the Allies was also brought to full status as a major element of Soviet propaganda on the war. This trend had been developing since 1946, and, like the other major elements of the Soviet interpretation of the war, had as its source Stalin's electoral speech of February 9, 1946. In this speech, Stalin had begun the process of depersonalizing Western policy that became so marked a characteristic of Soviet postwar historiography. "It would be incorrect to think," he had declared, "that the Second World War arose accidentally, or as the result of mistakes of one or another state figure. . . . As a matter of fact, the war arose as the inevitable result of the development of world economic and political forces on the basis of contemporary monopolistic capitalism."[15] Although he distinguished between the democratic and fascist states and acknowledged that the war against fascism was justified even before the Soviet Union entered it, his analysis of the contradictions of capitalism laid the basis for lumping all the capitalist states together in a common hostile category.

This spirit of the speech was reflected in the postwar propaganda treatment of the Allies. Beginning in 1946, mention of the Allies was dropped from the traditional Victory Day Order of the Day. At this time also, the delay in the second front began to be attributed to the machinations of Churchill.[16] In 1947, the anniversary of the German surrender to the Allies on May 8 was no longer observed, and the official celebration of this occasion was reserved for May 9, the anniversary of the surrender in Berlin, at which Soviet representatives participated. In 1948, increasing emphasis was placed on the anti-American line, and the whole policy of the Allies throughout the war was portrayed as deceitful and as hostile to the Soviet Union. The alleged military ineffectiveness of the Allies was also emphasized by derisive references to Churchill's request for Soviet assistance at the time of the Ardennes battle.[17]

To amplify this review of the development of postwar propaganda on the war, it will be useful to consider two political pamphlets that received broad dissemination at the time and that expressed more fully and clearly the trends reflected in the regular press articles. The first of these pamphlets was *The Great Fatherland War of the Soviet Union,* by the historian I. I. Mints, which was published in 1947 as a textbook for students in the Party political schools.[18] It represented the penultimate stage in the development of postwar historiography, a stage at which the full rigor of ideological interpretation had not yet quite blotted out all vestiges of realism. It was hyperbolic, inspirational, and full of the approved clichés, but it also contained features that were soon to become outdated. This may be seen both in its account of the military operations of the Soviet forces and in its treatment of the Allies.

In general, the military narrative was set in terms of the standard formulas. The doctrine of active defense was invoked to explain the early retreats. "The Red Army and Red Navy, in the period of the first battles of 1941, put into effect the Stalinist tactic of active defense and dispersed the Hitlerite's dreams of beating the Soviet Union in a few weeks."[19] Likewise, the victory below Moscow was presented as foreordained by Stalin's strategy. "The moment for the decisive counterblow for which the Red Army, in pursuance of the plan of its leader, Comrade Stalin, had long prepared, had matured."[20] The same line of interpretation was applied to Stalingrad. "The Stalingrad operation, conducted according to the plans and under the leadership of Comrade Stalin, was an incomparable example of military art."[21] Despite this orthodoxy, however, the text also contained elements that would be slightly out of harmony with the official mood a year or two later. Its reference to the Moscow crisis, for example, was more highly colored than would become customary in ordinary propaganda texts. "On October 19," the text read, "by decree of the State Defense Committee, the capital was declared in a state of siege. The workers of Moscow were called to active participation in the defense and to a merciless bringing to justice of provocateurs, spies, and other agents of the enemy."[22] Its acknowledgment of the role of the military leaders, though sparing, was more generous than customary. None was mentioned in connection with the Moscow battle, and only Chuikov, who was well down the line of command under Zhukov, Vasilevskiy, and Eremenko at Stalingrad, was mentioned in connection with this battle. Most of the major military leaders were mentioned, however, in connection with the operations of 1944 and 1945. This included Zhukov, although the sentence that included his name was the only one in the body of the text in which a marshal was cited without his title.[23] Zhukov was mentioned once again in an unusual accolade to the marshals given in the final summing up of the reasons for victory. "The Red Army had in its ranks leaders of a new type, commanders of the Stalinist military school—Marshals Vasilevskiy, Konev, Zhukov, Rokossovskiy, Voroshilov, Budennyy, Timoshenko, Govorov, Tolbukhin, Malinovskiy, Meretskov; outstanding generals, the front commanders Vatutin, Chernyakovskiy, Eremenko, Bagramyan, and others."[24]

Some imprecision was apparent also in the treatment of the Allies. The pamphlet contained, for example, the by now orthodox interpretation of Allied motives in delaying the second front. "The capitalists feared that the opening of a second front would hasten the defeat of Germany, that the Soviet Union would solidify its position and become stronger after a quick victory. They wished the Soviet Union to come out of the war weakened and exhausted,

and therefore Churchill delayed the opening of a second front."[25]
At the same time, the pamphlet gave a straightforward account of
the quick response of the U.S. and Great Britain to Russia's plight
in 1941, without deprecating their motives, although stress was
placed on the influence of public opinion in this action.[26] In one
reference, it hinted at the importance of Allied aid. It spoke of
the great significance of the defense of Murmansk, "through which
military supplies from the U.S.A. and England came to us."[27]

A much more rigidly doctrinaire interpretation of the Allied role
in the war, as well as of Soviet military operations, was given in
the second pamphlet. This also bore the title *The Great Patriotic
War of the Soviet Union* and was published in 1948, under Komsomol auspices, for students in the fourth term of the political
schools.[28] The importance of this pamphlet for Soviet internal
agitation work is indicated by the fact that it was published in hundreds of thousands of copies, in all the important republics of the
Soviet Union. It was written in very simple schoolbook language
and was obviously meant to summarize the essential theses on the
war that the Party wished to impress on the younger generation.

Except for giving Stalin exclusive credit, and except for not mentioning the marshals either individually or collectively, the account
of military operations in the pamphlet did not differ from what
had appeared before. The main emphasis in the pamphlet was on
the ineradicable hostility of the capitalist world for the country
of socialism and on the manifestation of this hostility in the actions
of the Allies during World War II. They were charged with having
encouraged Germany to attack the Soviet Union, with dragging
out the war to exhaust the Soviet Union, and with dallying on the
Western front so that German divisions could be shifted against
the Soviet Union. In general, the impression was created that the
Allies were really on the side of Hitler, and even the formation of
the Anglo-Soviet-American coalition was explained simply as a
failure of "the plans of international imperialism to knock together
a single front of capitalist states against the Soviet state."[29]

The subsequent course of Soviet propaganda about the war, until Stalin's death, was largely a filling out and elaboration of the themes that had been set during these first few postwar years. Somewhat ironically, but logically from the Soviet point of view, it was precisely during this later period of substantive immobility that the greatest outpouring of propaganda on the history of the war took place. An accidental reason for this increased propaganda was the fact that fifth and tenth anniversaries of important events of the war began to come along at this time.

The articles published in 1949, on the occasion of Stalin's seventieth birthday, gave high authoritative formulation to the trends of interpretation that had developed over the previous several years. The articles by Voroshilov and Bulganin, which were devoted to Stalin's activities as a military leader, brought the glorification of Stalin's role in the war to its highest point of development. *Questions of History* later referred to these articles as among the basic sources on the history of the war (the other major sources being Stalin's *The Great Patriotic War of the Soviet Union,* and his electoral speech of 1946).[30] A rash of articles, and even a few brochures, on Western "falsifications of history" (following the formula of the Sovinform pamphlet *Falsificators of History,* which will be considered separately below) contributed further impetus to the anti-Western ideological line of Soviet propaganda. Perhaps because of the completeness of their effacement from the substantive history of the war, the marshals were allowed to make something of a comeback as authors of the traditional war-anniversary articles. The tendency to subordinate the observances of the war to the polemic uses of current policy became even more marked during the Korean War period. Finally, Stalin's *Economic Problems of Socialism,* which came out in the fall of 1952, contributed still further to the abstractness and ideological character of Soviet interpretations of Western policy during the war and prewar years.

A few illustrations from the materials of these years will show the nature of the elaborations they introduced into the history of the war. Most, if not all, of these elaborations were aimed at a further denigration of the Western role in the war. An article in *Questions of History,* for example, put together an amazing series of slanderous allegations regarding the quality of American troops and the American command in the Ardennes battle.[31] After charging that the Allies had deliberately "advertised" their intention to rest and regroup before the Siegfried Line to permit Germany to shift divisions to the Eastern front, and after dilating on the "stupefying" shock that the German attack had on the American command, the article added:

It is interesting to note that in these critical days the "100 per cent Americans" unexpectedly began to show attention to the Negroes. "The Supreme Command," writes Butcher, "felt it could not deprive the Negroes the opportunity to distinguish themselves in battle." Having gotten into a scrape, the conceited Yankees preferred to forget about "the noble burden of the white man" and transferred the "burden" to the Negroes. The 100,000 Negroes, who, on the word of the same Butcher, had up to that time served in the rear units of the American Army, were hastily formed into battalions and sent to the front.[32]

An even more atrocious example of this style of historiography was provided by a brochure published in 1953. This dealt with a variety of alleged Western falsifications regarding the second front, the turning point of the war, and the role of the U.S.S.R. in the victories over Germany and Japan. The most serious charge made in the booklet was that the Allies deliberately sabotaged the supply of Russia over the Murmansk route by allowing their ships to be sunk. This is what it said:

In June–July, 1942, when the Soviet Union, because of the evacuation of a large part of its industry to the eastern regions, had experienced serious difficulties in supplying the army with all needs, a large number of transport ships coming to the U.S.S.R. were sunk. This happened because the English naval command intentionally divulged the time of departure of the convoy and the route it would follow, making this top-secret data available to the German fascist command. The ruling circles of the U.S.A. and England used the destruction of the transports to "prove" that dangers connected with the shipment of goods to the U.S.S.R. were too great and on this pretext curtailed the already miserable supplies.[33]

It is appropriate to conclude this review of the development of Soviet propaganda on the war at this point, since after 1953 new trends began to appear that will be discussed in a later chapter. Let us turn now to a consideration of some of the special devices used by the Party in the postwar period to dramatize or underline particular elements of its interpretation of the war.

STALIN'S LETTER TO COLONEL RAZIN

Stalin's letter to Colonel Razin was one of the most important events shaping the Soviet historical interpretation of World War II.[34] Ostensibly, the letter was an arbitrament of a dispute among professors at the Frunze and Voroshilov military academies regarding the merits of Clausewitz as an authority on military history and theory. The question was of some ideological significance, because Lenin's frequent citations of Clausewitz had appeared to give the latter a posthumous Marxist status. Stalin overcame this difficulty by pointing out that Lenin's use of Clausewitz for political purposes did not imply a general approbation of Clausewitz' philosophy or military and historical judgment. Moreover, in a carefully contrived assertion of his own pre-eminence over the fathers of Marxism, Stalin said that Lenin was not an expert on military affairs and that Engels was mistaken in accepting Clausewitz' evaluation of Barclay de Tolly as the best Russian general during the Napoleonic war. After this mighty fillip to the development of his own personality cult and to the chauvinistic trend of Soviet postwar propaganda, Stalin turned to the most significant point of his letter, the doctrine of the counteroffensive.

In the course of criticizing Colonel Razin's theses on war, Stalin made the following observation:

There is missing a section on the *counteroffensive* (not to be confused with the counterattack). I speak of a counteroffensive after a successful offensive by the enemy, which does not, however, bring decisive results, and in the course of which the defending side gathers its forces and goes over to a counteroffensive and administers a decisive defeat to the adversary. I think that a well-organized counteroffensive is a very interesting kind of offensive. To you as a historian it would be appropriate to interest yourself in these matters. The ancient Parthians knew about such a counteroffensive when they drew the Roman general Crassus and his army into the depths of their country and then striking in a counteroffensive, destroyed them. Our gifted General Kutuzov, who destroyed Napoleon and his army with the help of a well-prepared counteroffensive, also knew this well.[35]

This dilation on the strategy of planned retreat and the counteroffensive was the more striking and impressive because of the way in which it was presented. Stalin underlined the word "counteroffensive" when he first used it and warned against confusing it with the counterattack. He gave it further emphasis and effect by placing this little essay at the end of his letter and by disdaining to mention his own application of the feats of the Parthians and Kutuzov. Moreover, by speaking of the counteroffensive as "interesting," he unmistakably projected an image of himself as one who had devoted years to the profound study of military theory. This pose was further reinforced by his slighting reference to Lenin's military knowledge, when he mentioned Lenin's adjuration to "us then still young comrades from the *Tseka* [Central Committee] 'to study military matters thoroughly.'"

The main purpose of the letter was obviously to provide an additional theory, more sophisticated than the active-defense doctrine, to help explain the early defeats of the war and, at the same time, to magnify Stalin's military leadership. Stalin's description of the counteroffensive as a "kind of offensive" was very important in this regard. The word counteroffensive was hardly ever mentioned in subsequent articles without this phrase tacked on as a descriptive qualification. The effect of Stalin's letter on the interpretation of the war was made evident very quickly in the reactions of historians and propagandists. Some indication of this has already been given. A few other notable examples of the impact of this doctrine on the historiography of the war will be mentioned briefly here.

A fifth anniversary article, "The Great Stalingrad Battle," by B. Telpukhovskiy, which was the first full-scale article on the war to appear in *Questions of History* in the postwar period, provided an extended gloss on this theory.[36] It made clear that the more remote historical implications of Stalin's letter were subordinate to its implications for the interpretation of World War II.

This problem [i.e., the counteroffensive] in its whole range, both in its practical and theoretical aspects, was established only by the Red Army under the leadership of J. V. Stalin during World War II. Thus, J. V. Stalin, in responding to the letter of Colonel Razin, pointed particularly to the importance of studying the previous experience of the conduct of the counteroffensive and the importance of the theoretical mastery of it as a strategic form of waging war.[37]

The counteroffensive doctrine occupied a prominent place in certain of the authoritative articles on the history of the war that were published in honor of Stalin's seventieth birthday. Voroshilov, for example, in an article that elaborated the distinction between military science and military art, as Bulganin had done on the Armed Forces anniversary of the year before, made special mention "of so decisive a form of waging war as the strategic counteroffensive, with which the Soviet armed forces took over the strategic initiative in the early stage of the war despite the adversary's overwhelming superiority in forces and resources."[38] Bulganin discussed the doctrine more eloquently.

Knowing that there were great reserves near Moscow at the disposal of Headquarters, the Supreme Command of the Western front [i.e., either Timoshenko or Zhukov] made requests for reinforcements. Comrade Stalin demanded, however, that the enemy be checked with the forces on hand. The wisdom of Stalin's decision soon became apparent. Comrade Stalin kept his reserves for the transition to a decisive counteroffensive. . . . Comrade Stalin personally directed the whole course of every operation. Each day, and even several times a day, he verified the fulfillment of his orders, gave advice, and corrected the decisions of those in command if necessary. . . . Comrade Stalin's development of the questions of active defense and the counteroffensive is an outstanding service with respect to military theory.[39]

Marshal Vasilevskiy, at the Nineteenth Party Congress, went one step further and spoke about the counteroffensive as a strategy for a future war. "The Soviet Army is also successfully mastering the preparation and waging of that important kind of offensive developed by the greatest commander, Comrade Stalin—the counteroffensive."[40] This list of quotations could be extended almost indefinitely.

One of the most striking illustrations of the far-reaching effects of the doctrine of the counteroffensive was the impact it had on the historical evaluation of Kutuzov, whom Stalin had, in effect, made a military prototype of himself. Beginning immediately after Stalin's letter to Razin, a series of book reviews, published in *Questions of History* and elsewhere, revealed that the official interpretation of Kutuzov had undergone a fundamental reorientation in line with Stalin's remarks. The most prominent victim of this reorientation was the historian Tarlé, whose book *Napoleon's Invasion of Russia,* first published in 1939, was subjected to official rebuke in *Bolshevik* in 1951.[41] While the motives for the criticism of Tarlé were mixed and included the purely chauvinist desire to enhance the distinctively Russian factors in the defeat of Napoleon as against interpretations that had given major credit to foreign generals in the Russian Army, it became clear that the regime was using the Tarlé affair to write the history of World War II in palimpsest, as it were, over the history of the events of 150 years before, and that Kutuzov had been made a surrogate of Stalin's military reputation. In the original attack on Tarlé, the *Bolshevik* article recalled Stalin's statement that Kutuzov had defeated Napoleon by a well-prepared counteroffensive. It continued: "An objective study of the data on 1812, both published and archival, exposes the antiscientific nature of Tarlé's conception [that Kutuzov was reluctant to give battle] and shows that it was Kutuzov who destroyed Napoleon's army by a well-prepared counteroffensive and by bold pursuit of the enemy along a line parallel to his line of retreat."[42]

The close connection of the affair to the historical interpretation of World War II was made even clearer by Tarlé in his reply to *Bolshevik*. Pointing out that he was engaged in writing a new book on the invasion of 1812, Tarlé attempted to explain how it would differ from the old.

First and foremost [he said] is the fact that it is being written after the Great Patriotic War, after the glorious victory of 1945. Certainly, it is no longer possible to view much of our past history generally, and our military history in particular, in the same light as we viewed it before the world historic changes that followed from our 1945 victory, unprecedented as it was in scope and significance. . . . Moreover, I will come to the main point. In my new book I am disclosing something that was not shown in my old book: the great (and brilliantly executed) strategic calculation that led Kutuzov, first, to the decision to offer a major battle at Borodino, and then included the plan for the counteroffensive, which in my new book will occupy its due place for the first time.[43]

In its second attack, brought about by Tarlé's refusal to make an unqualified recantation, *Bolshevik* returned to the issue of the counteroffensive. Again, the parallelism between the disputed issue and the events of 1941–42 was clearly disclosed.

Academician Tarlé's mistake consists in the fact that he separated the
patriotic struggle of the peasantry against the invaders from the actions of the Russian Army. As before, he underestimates the decisive
significance of the military operations of the Russian Army and of
Kutuzov's active strategy and sees the decisive cause of the ruin of
Napoleon's army only in the elemental struggle of the Russian peasantry. However, Kutuzov, like a true great commander [here we can
almost hear Bulganin's and Voroshilov's disquisitions on military sci-
ence], both in working out the strategic plan of the counteroffensive
and in brilliantly carrying it out, not only took into account the selfless
struggle of the masses but also in every possible way fostered its development and relied on it as an important factor in defeating the army
of the aggressor.[44]

Tarlé finally made his recantation, although in his own way,
without abject contrition, in an article, published in *Questions of
History* in 1952. In it, he again made clear his understanding that
the Party's criticism had been motivated in large part by the desire
to make the events of 1812 a prefigure of the events of 1941–42.
"Before the well-known instructions of J. V. Stalin," he said, "the
whole War of 1812 . . . was not considered as the realization of a
deep plan of Kutuzov—a plan for the preparation and then the
realization of an unbroken counteroffensive."[45] His new book, he
said, would give him the opportunity to correct and amplify his
previous conception and to attempt to present to the Soviet reader
the history of 1812 "on the basis of the existing methodological
instructions, proceeding from that strategy, which, in the eyes of
our generation, led the army of the Soviet Union to the greatest
victory in world history."[46] He did not, he said, ever ascribe to
hunger or cold the significance of factors determining the outcome
of the war; but if among certain readers such a misconception
could arise, then it would be necessary to expound his thought
more exactly. "I will formulate it now thus: The strategy of Kutuzov led to Borodino and then created a profoundly conceived

and unusually skillfully conducted counteroffensive 'that destroyed Napoleon.' "[47]

THE CRITICISM OF FADEYEV'S *The Young Guard*

A very important feature of the postwar propaganda on the war was the claim that the Party had "always and everywhere" inspired and led the people's resistance to the Germans. This claim was advanced particularly, but by no means exclusively, with respect to the civilian aspects of the wartime achievements—the evacuation of industry to the east, the feats of labor heroism performed at the rear, the partisan war carried on behind enemy lines. The presentation of the Party's role in the war suffered somewhat at that time as a result of the natural concentration of the press on military affairs. A strong reaffirmation of the Party's central place in the wartime achievements was to be expected, therefore, after the war, and this was achieved most dramatically by the official criticism of Fadeyev's novel *The Young Guard,* published in 1945.

The effect of the criticism was all the greater because of the high standing Fadeyev enjoyed in the Soviet official and literary hierarchy and by the popularity of the novel, which had won a Stalin Prize. Fadeyev had headed the board of the Union of Soviet Writers from 1938 to 1944, and, after a brief interlude, had been reappointed to that position in 1946 by the same Party decree that had opened the postwar ideological campaign by its attack on the journals *Leningrad* and *Zvezda*. The redesignation of his post in this same decree as "General Secretary" of the board, a name similar to Stalin's title as head of the Communist Party, emphasized Fadeyev's unique status as a little Stalin of the literary hierarchy.

The subject of *The Young Guard* was a partisan youth group in the town of Krasnodon, in the Ukraine, during the German occupation. Its theme was the courage and initiative displayed by Soviet youth when thrown on their own resources. The story was based on actual events and most of the characters in the novel had their real-life counterparts. An article that appeared in *VOKS Bulletin,* in 1948, tells how the idea for the novel was conceived and how it was written.[48] Shortly after the liberation of Krasnodon in 1943, an army correspondent informed the Komsomol Central Committee that traces of a youth movement had been found in the town. A commission was sent to investigate, and as a result of their researches, a three-volume dossier of documents, photographs, interviews with townspeople, etc., was prepared on the subject. This provided the basis for posthumous awards of Hero of the Soviet Union to five members of the Young Guard, the name of the youth movement, and for a great propaganda fanfare about their feats in the Soviet press. But, according to the VOKS account, it was felt that the other members of the Young Guard also deserved to have their feats immortalized, and writers were asked to record the history of the group. Fadeyev accepted the assignment, and after further personal on-the-spot investigation, turned out the novel in a year and nine months.

The first criticism of the novel appeared in *Culture and Life,* the Central Committee's ideological organ, in November, 1947, and was followed up a few days later by a similar article in *Pravda.*[49] By the standards of the time, the criticism was not severe and did not bring about either a direct condemnation of the book or administrative punishment of Fadeyev personally. However, it had a sharp impact on the literary community, for writers knew that it constituted a clear directive on the interpretation of the war; thus it led to similar criticisms of other war novels.[50] The criticism was directed formally at the staging of the novel as a play, but the real target was the novel itself.

The substance of the criticism was that the novel failed to show "the leading activity of Party organizations" in the underground. "This creates the incorrect idea," declared *Culture and Life,* "that the Komsomols of Krasnodon acted spontaneously, that they did not feel the directing hand of the Bolshevik underground organization, that they were not a detachment of a single, powerful, and integrated army, but were a sort of isolated group of enthusiasts." Moreover, by depicting the evacuation of Krasnodon in the face of the German invasion as a chaotic rout, the novel sinned against historical truth and maligned the great organizing achievements of the Communist Party. "Certainly, not all went smoothly; there were failures and all kinds of unforeseen circumstances arose, but Bolshevik strength, reason, and organizational ability invariably conquered." Generalizing these observations into a rule, *Pravda* proclaimed the impossibility, without sinning against historical and artistic truth, of depicting a Komsomol organization divorced from the Party. "The Party everywhere and always introduced an organizing basis. Communists did not for a minute lose the leading role."

The real significance of this criticism was revealed years later by one who was in a position to know better than almost anyone else what it meant to the Soviet writers. Konstantin Simonov, a friend of Fadeyev and one of his lieutenants during those years, writing in *New World* in 1956, spoke of it as "the one postwar criticism that caused me to feel the greatest inner revulsion."

The criticism of the novel *The Young Guard* set forth many standardizing requirements, directed not only at this novel but at literature as a whole, because this article (the story of whose appearance is widely known) was extensively treated—unjustifiably, we might add—as the Party's viewpoint on the tasks of literature, and, first and foremost, on the description of the era of the Great Patriotic War. This version of the organized character of the beginning period of the war, and of the evacuation—and this "everywhere and at all places"—led to innumerable distortions of historical truth in many works. At the same time, this version forced many artists who had personally witnessed the war to give up the idea of writing about its first stage. It made them set aside their creative plans and go on to other subjects, sometimes less close to them. They did not want to compromise their consciences by depicting the first stage of the war according to the standardized requirements expressed in this article and, later, in many other articles. All this, of course, caused serious harm to literature, preventing it from expressing the entire tragic grandeur of the Patriotic War, and the full measure of heroism of the Party and the people. . . .

It is not by chance that Fadeyev spent exactly four years creating the revision of his novel, on the few chapters that he added to it. For him, as an honest artist, this work was painful and difficult. He knew, and this was not a secret, that the directions for this article had been given by J. V. Stalin himself.[51]

THE FALSIFICATORS OF HISTORY

A third event that had great influence in defining the Soviet official version of the war was the publication by the Soviet Information Bureau, in 1948, of a booklet entitled *Falsificators of History*.[52] This booklet was expressly designed as a rebuttal to the State Department publication, *Nazi-Soviet Relations, 1939–1941*, and was in part an introductory commentary to a collection of German documents that had been captured by the Soviet Army and was published shortly thereafter under the title *Documents and Materials Relating to the Eve of the Second World War*.[53] Needless to say, the documents that appeared in this publication were selected to place the prewar diplomacy of the Western states in a discreditable light. From the time of their publication, the *Falsificators of History* pamphlet and its supporting documents became the single most important source of Soviet historical writing on the war period and provided a definitive framework for the interpretation of the Western role in the war.

In line with its polemic character, *Falsificators of History*, like the State Department publication against which it was directed, was focused on the diplomatic prehistory of the war. However, the scope of this coverage was broadened to include, on the one hand, the whole course of the breakdown of the Versailles system and the rise of Hitler to international power, and, on the other, the actions of the Allies during the war itself. After a running start

with an account of the re-establishment of German war industry
with the help of American loans, the pamphlet settled down to a
more detailed indictment of the Western policy of appeasement.
The Western leaders were represented as working to buy their own
security by sacrificing small states and by encouraging Hitler to
satisfy his expansionist ambitions in eastern Europe. This policy
culminated in the "unheard-of treachery" of Munich, which, "far
from being a chance episode in the policy of these states, represented a highly important phase in their policy aimed at goading
the Hitlerite aggressors against the Soviet Union."[54] Likewise,
according to the pamphlet, the Anglo-French negotiations with the
Soviet Union in 1939 were, from the very beginning, "nothing but
another move in their double game."[55] Proof of this were the negotiations for a broad political understanding between England and
Germany that were being carried on in July and August by Mr.
Wilson, a British cabinet official and intimate of Chamberlain,
and Herr Wohltat, the German Commissioner for the Four-Year
Plan. In view of all this, according to the pamphlet, the Soviet
Union had no alternative but to sign a nonaggression pact with
Hitler and, by diplomatic and military means, to erect an "eastern
front" against German aggression. Finally, concluded the pamphlet,
during the war, the double game of the Allies continued. Incidents
in this game were the secret contacts established between the Allies
and Germany in Lisbon (Aitken–von Koerver) and in Switzerland
(Dulles-Hohenlohe) and the delay of the second front.

As the above summary suggests, the argumentation presented in
Falsificators of History was highly tendentious. This effect was
achieved not by falsification of evidence but by a narrow selection
of documents and by a strained interpretation of the documents
selected. Illustrative in this connection was the treatment of the
conversation between Halifax and Hitler on November 19, 1937,
in which Lord Halifax urged a British-German understanding as
a first step toward a broader European settlement. "After the
ground is prepared by Anglo-German *rapprochement*," he said,

"the four great West European powers must jointly set up the foundations for lasting peace in Europe."[56] In commenting on this proposal, *Falsificators of History* concluded: "In other words, Halifax, as far back as 1937, had proposed to Hitler on behalf of the British Government that Britain as well as France should join the Berlin-Rome Axis."[57] Another example of the *Falsificators of History* method is provided by the same conversation. Halifax, acknowledging that changes affecting the status of Danzig, Austria, and Czechoslovakia would probably take place in any event sooner or later, stated: "England is only interested that these changes should be effected by peaceful evolution, so as to avoid methods which may cause further convulsions, undesired either by the Fuehrer or by other countries."[58] This observation of Halifax, in the interpretation of the pamphlet, was evidence "that the British Government viewed favorably Hitler's plans for the 'acquisition' of Danzig, Austria, and Czechoslovakia." Also, according to the pamphlet: "It was a deal, a secret agreement of the British Government with Hitler about satisfying the annexationist appetites of the latter at the expense of third countries.[59] Another example is afforded by the uncritical treatment given to the documents originating from the German Ambassador in London, Dirksen, whose reports were colored by his personal adherence to a policy of Anglo-German *rapprochement*.[60] Thus, for example, the pamphlet accepted Dirksen's report that the British Government had "come nearer to understanding the demands of Germany and was ready to make great sacrifices to meet them" as one element of proof that "between the British Government and Hitler there was indeed established a far-reaching accord in foreign-policy plans."[61] These examples are fairly typical of the technique of exposition followed in *Falsificators of History*.

The significance of this pamphlet was immediately reflected in the effect it had on subsequent historical writing. Its concepts, its data, even its phraseology became the basic grist of historiography on the Allied role in the war. It marked a dramatic reaffirmation of the analysis of Western policy given by Stalin in his report to the Eighteenth Party Congress in 1939.

The policy of nonintervention means conniving at aggression, giving free rein to war, and consequently transforming the war into a world war. The policy of nonintervention reveals an eagerness, a desire . . . to allow all belligerents to sink deeply into the mire of war; to encourage them surreptitiously in this direction; to allow them to weaken and exhaust one another; and then, when they have become weak enough, to appear on the scene with fresh strength, to appear, of course, in the "interests of peace," and to dictate conditions to the enfeebled belligerents.[62]

It also marked the definite end of the lingering restraint that the Soviet Union had shown in including the U.S. under the full opprobrium of blame already heaped on the other Allies.

It was customary until lately to consider that the entire responsibility for the Munich policy of treachery rests with the ruling circles of Britain and France, with the governments of Chamberlain and Daladier.

The fact that the American Government undertook to make the German files public, while excluding the documents pertaining to the Munich agreement, shows that the United States Government is interested in whitewashing the heroes of the Munich treachery and in putting the blame on the U.S.S.R.[63]

Henceforth, the U.S. would not only share the blame with the other Allies, but would become the chief culprit in the Soviet historical indictment of the Allied role in the war.

The Military and the Interpretation of the War

Alongside the public account of the war propagated in the media of mass communication, a more specialized literature, authored by experienced military officers, made its appearance in the professional military journals. The best of this writing was published in *Military Thought,* the General Staff journal, which, during most of the Stalinist postwar period, was designed for a restricted military readership. This literature was as deeply affected by the postwar political climate as the public propaganda and displayed many of the features of artificiality characteristic of the latter. But it also provided some insights into the military's true appraisal of the war. In particular, it showed that military officers felt some disdain for the idealizations of World War II history in which they were required to express their experience of the wartime events.

THE CONTRIBUTION OF THE MILITARY TO THE OFFICIAL LINE ON THE WAR

Although *Military Thought* is written by and for professional officers and provides a forum for exchanges of view on technical military matters, it is essentially a theoretical publication whose primary function during the postwar Stalin period was to keep military theory in line with Party and state policy. It was published by the Historical Administration of the General Staff, and its editorial policy was set by a small group of staff officers and military professors who specialized in theoretical matters. Prominent among them were Major General N. Talenskiy, who was editor of the journal from 1945 to 1954; Major General N. Zamyatin, a member of the editorial board; and Major General M. Galaktionov, who acted as military analyst for *Pravda*. Their positions and functions gave these men a very strong influence on the way military questions were interpreted in other official publications. As will be seen, the views promoted by *Military Thought* on a number of questions affecting the interpretation of the war exercised a strong influence on the official version of this event.

The whole complex of doctrines affecting the interpretation of the defensive period of Soviet operations—active defense, the foresight of the Supreme Command, the timely concentration of reserves, the counteroffensive, etc.—were all fully elaborated in *Military Thought* before they achieved a comparable formularization in public propaganda. Indeed, the origins of Soviet military views on many of these questions go back to the prewar period, when Soviet theorists were following the course of military events in Europe to draw what conclusions they could for their own uses. Soviet officers appeared to be favorably impressed, for example, with the plans developed by the French General Weygand for coping with German blitzkrieg tactics, and they apparently believed that the same methods could be applied in Russia.[1] The tendency of Soviet theory to take the wish for the deed may explain why, when it became necessary for Soviet theorists to explain what had happened on the Soviet-German front, they tended to see the outlines of these ideal prescriptions in the actual behavior of the Soviet Army during this period.

From very early in the war, articles in *Military Thought* lay stress on the activeness, flexibility, and maneuvering character of Soviet defensive tactics. The theory of "active defense," or, as it was often called in military literature, "strategic defense," was regularly used as descriptive of the early period of military operations and was presented as an inherently transitional stage, looking toward a counteroffensive. Major General Galaktionov, for example, in an article in 1943, treated the doctrine in this way.

The strategic defense of the Red Army included the idea of activeness at its basis, the idea of a transition to offensive action. It is not at all accidental that the periods of strategic defense were completed by the transition of our troops to the offensive. The task of strategic defense consists in stopping, wearing down, and bleeding white the enemy, and thus preparing his defeat, which is completed by a transition to the offensive. In the course of defensive actions, the Soviet command planned the offensive operations, concentrating strategic reserves in areas from which powerful blows could be launched on the enemy.[2]

By 1945, at least, the ideas underlying the "strategic defense" and "counteroffensive" concepts had been developed into a fully elaborated theoretical system. In an article entitled "Strategic Objective," Major General Galaktionov attempted to show, with particular reference to Stalingrad, how Stalin's strategic calculations had dominated and defined the course of military operations during the first two years of war and had led to decisive victorious results.[3] His main point, premised on the theoretical argument that the defending side as well as the attacking side could set a strategic objective, was that the Soviet command (i.e., Stalin) had conceived the outline of the subsequent offensive operations during the course of the defensive battles of 1941 and 1942, and that it had orchestrated all plans to harmonize with this conception. There were three phases, he said, in the development and unfolding of the commander's strategy: first, the discernment of the enemy's intentions; second, the adoption of a defensive plan; and third, the announcement to the troops of a definite strategic objective (i.e., a plan for the decisive defeat of the enemy). Somewhere between the first and second phases, said Galaktionov, the germ of the subsequent offensive operation was present in the mind of the commander. Obviously, this theoretical framework, smacking strongly of a kind of Tolstoyan mysticism, provided unlimited opportunities for propagating the myth of Stalin's clairvoyance as a military commander.

In applying this theory to the interpretation of the first year of the war, Galaktionov pretended to see the outlines of the December counteroffensive already present in the planning of the Supreme Command as early as July. This he found in the "most revealing index" of the intentions and actions of any high command—"the disposal it makes of its strategic reserves." By dispatching some of its reserves to Smolensk, said Galaktionov, the Supreme Command defined the main direction on which defensive efforts were to be concentrated. Although this did not mean that the Supreme Command could already foresee the emergence of German tanks in the vicinity of Moscow, it did mean that the "guiding strategic idea," which found its final expression in the December counteroffensive, was already clearly apparent in the battle of Smolensk. "Consequently, in the second phase, the Soviet Command already carried out a definite plan. Although the strategic objective could not yet be pointed out to the troops, its germ was already contained in this plan and subsequently grew out of it."[4]

Galaktionov's account of the Stalingrad battle was similar, but even more elaborate. To reconcile the account with the official dictum that the encirclement of Moscow had been the Germans' objective, Galaktionov described Stalingrad as the "center of gravity" of the 1942 operations, the mid-point between the strategic objective of the attacking side and the strategic objective of the defending side. Again, this time as early as August, he claimed to see the outline of the subsequent counteroffensive already present in the defensive plans of the Supreme Command.

"Give me a place to stand, and I will move the world," said Archimedes. To direct the events of the summer of 1942, the Commander in Chief had need of a fulcrum. Stalingrad served this purpose. At the leader's word it was created by the heroes of the Stalingrad defense. The center of gravity of the struggle was shifted here. A firm foundation was created for elaborating and carrying out Stalin's brilliant plan.[5]

The obvious similarity of these ideas to the concepts that were later officially formulated in the doctrine of the counteroffensive was further underlined by Galaktionov's application of them, in his introductory paragraphs, to an analysis of Kutuzov's strategy in 1812. All of this strongly suggests that Galaktionov was one of the inspirers of the views expressed by Stalin in his letter to Colonel Razin in 1947.

An even more direct inspiration of Stalin's letter, and of the whole doctrine of the counteroffensive, was an article entitled "The Strategic Counteroffensive," by Major General Talenskiy, which was published in *Military Thought* in 1946.[6] Every element of Stalin's later doctrine on the counteroffensive was present in this article. It defined the counteroffensive essentially as Stalin later did, although somewhat more wordily.

[The counteroffensive is] an organized aggregate of operations of strategic significance, immediately following operations of strategic defense, and aimed at seizing the operational and strategic initiative from the hands of the adversary, weakened by the preceding defensive operations . . . and thus at creating the necessary conditions and laying the basis for a general strategic offensive, with the task of winning the campaign and, in certain cases, the war as a whole.[7]

It invoked the same historical examples. "In the year 53 our era, the Roman commander Marcus Licinius Crassus was met with such a strategy by the Parthians against whom he was waging war. . . . The defense and counteroffensive were joined still more notably in the strategy of Kutuzov in 1812."[8] Finally, the significance of the doctrine for the interpretation of World War II was clearly indicated. "The strategic counteroffensive, as an active form of struggle, which is inseparably combined with the strategic defense and crowns it, received clear formulation in the command activities of Comrade Stalin in the period of the Civil War, and it received further development in the Great Patriotic War of 1941–45."[9] The directive nature of the article was explicit. "The examples of the strategic counteroffensive created by Comrade Stalin in the course of the Great Patriotic War are the greatest contribution to military science. A further theoretical working out of this strategic form of waging war and its practical mastery by the military leaders of our armed forces is necessary."[10]

Further evidence of the influence of *Military Thought* on the formulation of Stalin's views on the counteroffensive, and on the role of Kutuzov, is afforded by the early activity of this journal in the history of the War of 1812. For example, two articles on this subject appeared together in 1945, one by Lieutenant Colonel Meshcheryakov, presenting a blunt and categorical attack on Clausewitz as an idealogue of Prussian reactionism,[11] and another by Professor N. Korobkov, denouncing past historical belittlements of Kutuzov.[12] Another article, in 1946, by Major R. Rozhkov, presented a direct criticism of Tarlé for his interpretation of Kutuzov's strategy.[13] Throughout the postwar period, military historians continued to take a proprietary interest in the subject of Kutuzov studies, and, as Tarlé later seemed to acknowledge, they were the recognized authorities in this field.[14]

Military Thought appeared to be "more royalist than the king" in other aspects of the interpretation of the war as well. Its victory editorial, for example, contained a foreshadowing of Stalin's speech to the electors in its assertion that the war had represented a successful test of the prewar policies of the Party.[15] It sought to drive home the lesson that the Soviet regime had corrected the mistakes of the Czarist regime and had seen to it that the Soviet country had the means to defend itself when the great test came. *Military Thought*'s attitude toward the Allies, after a period of wartime generosity, cooled at least as rapidly as public propaganda in this field. While there was still some objectivity, if not warmth, in treatments of the Allies in 1945, by 1946 the intrusion of the propaganda hand in these accounts had become manifest.[16] Finally, its praise of Stalin was slavish and unlimited. The character of this aspect of *Military Thought* in the postwar period is perhaps best summarized in the self-criticism the editors themselves made after Stalin's death. "It is necessary to say outright that, in respect to the cult of personality, there is not a single science that has been harmed as much as military science."[17]

These illustrations show that the most distinctive features of the official interpretation of the military operations of the war were developed in *Military Thought* before they became a part of official propaganda. This points to the key role of the Historical Administration of the General Staff in shaping the official interpretation of the war. The most striking indication of this influence was the direct inspiration provided by *Military Thought* for the ideas contained in Stalin's letter to Razin and for the whole elaborate structure of interpretations surrounding the theory of the counteroffensive. The professional military theorists, it is clear, produced the ideas and the technical verbiage that permitted Soviet propaganda to present the course of defensive operations during the early period of the war in plausibly favorable terms. In the following sections, we will consider *Military Thought* from another angle—to see whether the strong idealizing tendency of its editorial policy obscured all elements of realism and professional independence in the accounts of the war appearing in its pages. We will pursue this line of inquiry first with respect to the articles that appeared during the war itself.

ELEMENTS OF REALISM IN THE WARTIME ACCOUNTS

Military Thought was never free—not even during the war— from influences that tended to idealize Soviet military performance.

Although the journal was intended for a professional audience, and was specifically limited to that audience shortly after the war, it was not so closely restricted that considerations of officer morale could be neglected. Moreover, Soviet officers had the normal tendency to present their own performance in the best possible light. Despite these official and natural human restraints, however, military writers produced articles during the war that showed they were fully alive to the shortcomings of the Soviet military performance and to the real nature of the events taking place at the front.

Elements of truth in the wartime accounts were generally of two kinds: acknowledgments of Soviet failures, and admissions that factors other than Soviet staunchness and military skill had some real effect in stopping the Germans. In addition, there were cases when the credit one would normally expect to be attributed to Stalin for military successes was toned down or even withheld. Of these categories of truth, the first was most common, being met with in the regular analyses of tactical operations that were presented as object lessons for commanders. An example of this kind of instructional literature was an article, in 1942, that described experiences on the Southwestern front to show typical German tactics in liquidating Russian break-throughs. Another, in 1944, that analyzed the Kursk battle, mentioned cases to illustrate the danger of tanks being cut off from their accompanying infantry.[18] Articles of this kind, being clearly intended for instructional purposes, of course, told nothing of the attitude of the authors toward the interpretation of the war as a whole.

More interesting in this respect were acknowledgments that Soviet troops had suffered general operational failure. Several examples of this were contained in an article by Lieutenant General Shilovskiy, in 1943, entitled "Growth of the Military Art of the Red Army in the Course of the Patriotic War."[19] He said the following regarding the Soviet operations below Moscow: "The troops mastered and successfully applied mainly the more simple methods

of operations; more complex methods—operations of encirclement, deep penetrations—were less successful, and sometimes
failed completely."[20] Again, regarding the quality of operational
command in the early period of the war, he said: "Decisive objectives were set as soon as possible before the beginning of operations. Sometimes, the scope of these objectives exceeded available
forces and means. In the future, we learned better to match operational tasks with the forces available for their execution."[21] Further, he made a statement that appeared to contradict the spirit,
if not the letter, of current and subsequent propaganda on the character of the battle of Moscow. "A head-on battle [meeting en-
gagement] seldom arose, taking place primarily in connection with
a counterblow by the reserves on attacking troops that had broken
through into the depths of the defense."[22] Again, elaborating on
the reasons for the early operational failures, he said:

The peculiarity of the given period was that the assault groups had
as their basic element cavalry [cavalry divisions or corps], and tank
brigades [and infantry] were attached to the cavalry and helped it in
the execution of the task of developing successes. Such a composition
of assault groups naturally told on the character of their operations, on
the methods of waging battle.
    As a result of the limited quantity of assault groups, maneuvers for
the encirclement of the adversary required time and, in certain cases,
did not yield decisive results. When an encirclement of the troops of
the adversary was nevertheless effected, they often did not succeed in
completing it by a full defeat of the encircled troops because of the
weakness of the encircling units.[23]

    Finally, drawing conclusions from the experience of the first
year of the war, Shilovskiy said: "At the same time, it [the first
year of the war] revealed a number of shortcomings in the preparation of our troops that it was necessary to liquidate as quickly as
possible."[24]
    There were also occasional examples during this period of ref-

erences to accidental factors and German mistakes as playing a role in Soviet successes. Major General Galaktionov, for example, made some admissions of this kind in his article "Certain Characteristics of Contemporary War," which analyzed the reasons for the failure of the blitzkrieg in Russia.[25] His main points were that the expanses of Russia were too great, and German forces insufficient, to permit the achievement of the primary goal of blitzkrieg, the breakup of the front. "Such a task [the cutting up and pulverizing of the front] proved itself beyond the powers of the German Army, in the first place because it had to be effected in a theater of military operations of great scale, and in the second place because the strength of the Red Army was incomparably greater than the German command had estimated."[26] Galaktionov laid great stress, perhaps more wishfully than accurately, on the maneuvering character of Soviet defensive tactics, which allegedly placed the Germans under constant threat of being cut off from their own rear. This led, he said in a somewhat unusual statement, to the stopping of the German mechanized divisions by destruction, or "by lack of gas."[27] Finally, in summarizing the results of the 1941–42 campaign, Galaktionov came close to an evaluation that could be accepted by most Western military analysts. "The Germans' basic weakness," he declared, "consisted in the lack of sufficiently strong strategic echelons capable of deciding the outcome of the war before the Red Army had succeeded in re-establishing its defensive front." Thus, before the Germans, he concluded, stood only "inglorious ruin and the boundless Russian expanses."[28]

Finally, to complete this analysis of the realistic elements in *Military Thought*'s wartime articles, we will return to the Shilovskiy article mentioned earlier for an example of unusual reticence regarding Stalin's military leadership. This occurred in Shilovskiy's discussion of the Stalingrad battle. He nowhere stated explicitly that the operation was planned and conducted by Stalin. Whether he implied it is dubious, particularly since he referred to the commander of the operation without identifying him as Stalin. It seems at the least that he chose his language carefully so as to make it compatible with whatever turn the official mood might take with respect to the role of the marshals in the war. This is what he said:

The commander who, in the very difficult situation at the end of 1942 in the south, could conceive and effect such an operation, has made the greatest contribution to military science and enriched military art with a classic example of a modern offensive operation leading to the complete encirclement and destruction of a large grouping of picked hostile troops.[29]

That was all. In orthodox practice, a sentence such as this would invariably be followed by a direct identification of Stalin as the genius who had made this contribution to the art of war.

INDEPENDENT VIEWS IN THE POSTWAR PERIOD

As one might expect, candor and realism in accounts of the war appeared more frequently during the war itself than during the postwar period, when the idealizing policy of the military theorists had become firmly established. However, this later period also showed that the working military officers had drawn conclusions from their wartime experience that did not fully jibe with the standardized requirements of the theorists. Some of the articles that appeared during this period seemed to point to an underlying conflict between theory and experience in military thinking about the war.

One sign of this was the brief appearance after the war of what appeared to be a branch-of-service viewpoint among specialized military journals. This seemed to reflect not only natural pride of service, but also certain practical conclusions that military officers had drawn from the experience of their own services in the war. These practical conclusions, of course—insofar as they seemed to magnify the role of one arm at the expense of another—ran head-on into the reigning Soviet doctrine on the equal merit of all arms in combined arms battle.

A small unsigned article in *Military Thought* in the summer of 1945 drew attention to this phenomenon.[30] It took to task a number of specialized military journals for exaggerating the roles of their own services in the war and for neglecting the Soviet doctrine on the coordinated action of all arms. These journals, said the article, "raise the basic question of the military employment of their own forces in combined arms battle poorly or not at all, and sometimes, in interpreting the experience of the military operations of their forces, attribute to them an independent significance."[31] The Air Forces journal came in for particular criticism in this regard. Illustrating its point with a quotation from the journal that claimed that "aviation plays the basic role in the complete defeat of the adversary in the concluding stage of an operational breakthrough," *Military Thought* observed that the editors of the journal understood the bases of our operational art "in their own peculiar way." "How else is it possible to explain that a similar treatment of the role of aviation is repeated in a number of articles?"[32] Marshal Rotmistrov's article, in 1946, which attributed to tanks "the decisive force in the attack," provided another example of this conflict between experience and theory.[33]

A more interesting case was a somewhat crusty article by Major General A. Penchevskiy, "Concerning Operations for Encirclement and Operational Terminology," which disputed the concept of "internal and external fronts" in an encirclement operation.[34] This concept was already becoming part of the legend of the Stalingrad operation, where, it was claimed, an "external front" had been formed on the encircling ring to prevent a break-in by Manstein's relief column, as well as an "internal front" to prevent a breakout by von Paulus' army. The use of this concept to buttress the claim that Stalin always beat the enemy "for sure," foreseeing on a large scale all the countermeasures that the enemy might possibly undertake, gave it a political significance.[35] Penchevskiy's argument was that the terms "internal and external fronts" were purely artificial concepts, that they did not correspond to what actually happened in an encirclement operation. "In the planning of an operation," said Penchevskiy, "the forces and means of an army and front (fronts) are never under any circumstances divided between internal and external fronts (lines). They are divided according to operational objectives, and tasks are established by defined lines." He concluded with a blunt dismissal of the theory. "Our staffs never used such concepts as 'internal and external fronts'; they are useless, since they do not explain the essence of the operational maneuver."[36] This language carried clear overtones of the impatience of the experienced military officer with the abstractions of the theorists.

. A still more interesting case was an article by General of the Army Eremenko, entitled "Counterblows in a Contemporary Defensive Operation," which appeared in 1949.[37] This was a notable article, if for no other reason than that, at the height of the Stalin apotheosis, it mentioned Stalin only once—in the opening paragraph—and the adjective "Stalinist" once—in the last. Moreover, it dealt with the question of the counteroffensive in such a way as to obscure the role of the Supreme Commander in directing this operation and to enhance the role of army and front commanders. He accomplished this by attributing to the counterblow (i.e., an operation of an army or front, larger than a counterattack, and smaller than a counteroffensive) the crucial role in triggering the counteroffensive, specifically with reference to Moscow and Kursk. He spoke of the counterblows in these two battles as "turning into" counteroffensives. This phraseology was in itself not unorthodox, but Eremenko's point of reference made it appear that the army or front commander, who made the decision for a counterblow, was in effect the agent responsible for the counteroffensive. This, in the atmosphere of 1949, was perilously close to lèse-majesté.

There is evidence that the unorthodoxy of this article was the result not of careless writing but of blunt military honesty. Time and again, Eremenko missed the obvious opportunities to throw a sop to Stalin's vanity. Repeatedly, he spoke of the counteroffensive as "growing out of," or "developing from," the counterblows launched by "our troops," without mentioning that it was "organized" by Stalin, as good propaganda practice required. In one place he went even further and implicitly credited Zhukov with preparing the counteroffensive below Moscow.

The battle below Moscow provides examples of such counterblows, where they were organized by order of the Supreme Command of the forces of the Western front [i.e., Zhukov]. The troops of the Western front, having exhausted and bled white the grouping of the German troops operating on the Moscow direction, and having definitely stopped the offensive of the adversary, at the beginning of December, 1941, undertook strong counterblows on the right and left wings of the front against the striking groups of the Germans, aimed at embracing Moscow from north and south. The counterblows were effected by the forces of the defending troops and with powerful reserve groups organized in the rear by the Supreme Command, and concentrated on the flanks of the striking groups of the adversary. These counterblows were the culminating moment of the stubborn active defense of our troops below Moscow; they set the basis for the decisive counteroffensive of the Soviet Army, which was completed by the utter defeat of the largest groupings of the troops of the adversary, and which guaranteed a sharp turn in the strategic situation.[38]

That Zhukov's role in the Moscow counteroffensive, as described above, was no unusual case in Eremenko's mind was made clear later in his article when he discussed conditions governing the command decision to launch a counterblow. "A correct and well-grounded decision is possible," he said, "only when there is a correct understanding of the task set by the senior commander and a true evaluation of the operational situation."[39] Obviously, according to Eremenko, the decision for the counterblow (and hence implicitly for the counteroffensive that might grow out of it) was not the exclusive prerogative of the Supreme Commander.

The ideological lapses of this article were thrown into stronger relief by a vigorously orthodox article on the counteroffensive that Eremenko published later. It provided a whole catalogue of the standard formulas praising Stalin as the genius exponent of this strategy.

In the Great Patriotic War, the counteroffensive assumed a scale and significance unprecedented in the history of war. The counteroffensives of the Soviet Army, conducted under the leadership of Comrade Stalin, played not only the decisive role in the most important campaigns of the past war, but in a fundamental way defined its course and outcome as a whole.[40]

The spirit of this article contrasted so sharply with the earlier one that the conclusion seems inescapable that considerations of political discretion had prompted it.

In summing up this review of military writing on the war, we may observe, first, that the military historians played a key role in developing the distinctively military concepts of the official version of the war. Second, despite this, military writers as a whole did not abdicate their professional judgment and provided snatches of direct testimony on the real nature of the wartime events. Third, some faint signs of dissatisfaction with elements of the official line appeared among military writers during the postwar period. This expressed itself not in any open opposition or resistance to the official line, but in indications that the professional military officers were aware of the underlying tension that existed between their direct experience of the military events of the war and the theoretical formulas in which they were required to express them.

4

The Professional Historians
and the War

While the military historians were taking an early lead in developing and propagating the ideas that formed the framework of the official interpretation of the war, the civilian historians were being shunted into other activities. Plans by the historical institutes for extensive research in the history of the war were abruptly canceled in 1946. Thenceforth, historians who continued to work in the contemporary period devoted themselves mainly to diplomatic history and the events leading up to the war—areas that proved to be hazardous when the Soviet official attitude toward the West rapidly hardened in the postwar period. Some of these historians succumbed to official pressure; others maintained a vigorous resistance, demonstrating a courage in their conflicts with the regime that derived less from political conviction than from personal integrity and professional pride.

THE HISTORY THAT NEVER WAS

As the war was drawing to its close, there were clear signs that the historians were looking forward expectantly to a period of intense historical work on the momentous experiences that they had only recently lived through. Late in 1944, the Presidium of the Academy of Sciences, as part of its planning for the postwar period, heard a report by Vice President V. P. Volgin on the outlook in the field of history. As is often the case in the Soviet Union with a program that is destined to have directive force, the report was published for "broad discussion" among the interested scholars.[1] In form and substance, this report was a general plan for the guidance over the "next few years" of the institutes of the Academy engaged in historical studies. The most remarkable feature of the report, from the viewpoint of subsequent developments, was the degree to which it was dominated by the assumption that the war would occupy a central place in the future work of the historians.

Academician Volgin advanced, as the premise of his recommendations, the thought that the war, and the activities and institutions highlighted by it, would be the main subject of reader interest after the war. Consequently, every aspect of the war should be the subject of historical investigation. This would include, specifically, military history. In this connection, he said, "it is characteristic that corresponding sections, military-historical, have been organized in two of our institutes—the History Institute and the Institute of the History of Material Culture. These sections have already begun to work."[2]

The background of preparation that the historians had made for the postwar historical harvest was also revealed in this report. A group of historians, it was said, had begun to gather materials as early as 1942, and a formal commission, under the chairmanship of G. F. Aleksandrov, had been set up to prepare a "chronicle of the Great Patriotic War." To this end, a huge amount of material had been collected on the key episodes of the war, the partisan movement, the people's levy, the guards units, the lives of heroes of the Soviet Union, etc. This, said the reporter, with an enthusiasm that seemed to reflect the spirit of the times, "is only the beginning of a work that will attract many generations of historians, both in our country and beyond its borders."[3]

Approximately a year later, another article on the future plans of the History Institute showed that the war-end optimism of the historians had been premature. The article announced that the five-year plan of the History Institute, growing out of the 1944 report, had been "reconsidered in the light of the historical speech of Comrade Stalin of February 9, 1946." The revised plan, presented in this article, made no provision for work on World War II. Certain rubrics contained in the plan, such as "modern world history" and "Red Army history," were the closest it came to touching the subject of World War II.[4]

Somewhat later in the year, Professor Genkina, in a report to the Learned Council of the History Institute, gave some further clues as to the directions postwar historical work would take. The main conclusion of the report was that work on the institutional structure of the Soviet social and state system was of prime concern. Quoting the report of the jury of the government commission on the competition for the best textbook (1937) as relevant to present tasks, Genkina listed the "basic things" requiring historical elucidation: the socialization of industry, the nationalization of land, the federal constitution, the Soviet state system. At the end of the report, Genkina mentioned World War II almost reproachfully. "It is characteristic that considerably more has been done by our historians on the study of the Great Patriotic War than on the period of peaceful construction that preceded the war."[5]

The final clue to the fate of the long-anticipated historical work on World War II appeared in the spring of 1947. A report on the work of the contemporary history sector of the History Institute stated that the first volume of a "History of World War II" had been sent to the press.[6] What happened to it there is not known, but it was apparently never published. It was not mentioned again in *Questions of History* in the postwar period and no other record of it has been found.

This chronicle of frustrated hopes brings out vividly a fact that any major library catalogue might suggest—that from 1946 until near the end of Stalin's life, the history of World War II was virtually a forbidden topic for Soviet professional historians. Except for a fifth-anniversary article on the Stalingrad battle, written moreover by a military historian, no articles dealing directly on World War II appeared in *Questions of History* from the first issue of 1946 until the last issue of 1949, when the anniversary articles on Stalin's seventieth birthday reopened this subject. Academic research on World War II, judging by the reports of dissertations defended in Soviet universities that appeared from time to time in *Questions of History,* also virtually ceased during this period. A mere handful of dissertations on war topics were noted, all of candidate rank, and all dealing with local partisan work (except for the Academy of Social Sciences, where some work on international relations of the wartime period was sponsored). All of this negative evidence, pointing to the virtual abandonment of World War II history by Soviet historians, was directly confirmed by a review article in 1953, which described certain works appearing in 1951 and 1952 as "the first attempt" to give a short popular description of the events of the Great Patriotic War.[7]

It seems obvious that the history of World War II was looked upon by the regime as too sensitive a political topic to be entrusted to historians, at least during the period of postwar readjustment. This probably reflected not so much a mistrust of the historians—although during the early postwar period this may have been a factor—as a reluctance by the regime to stir up memories that could serve no useful political purpose. When attention to the war was resumed in the early 1950's, the relevance of this history to the current political objectives of vigilance and military preparedness was made clear.

DIPLOMATIC HISTORY AND INTERNATIONAL RELATIONS

Shut off from the military history of the war, the historians continuing to work on the wartime period turned their attention to the history of diplomacy and international affairs. Indeed, a fairly clearly defined division of effort took shape, with the military historians apparently assigned responsibility for the military history of the war and the civilian historians given rein in the diplomatic prehistory of the war. In the work of the latter, there was considerable variety of tone and style during the first few postwar years. A number of historians—and they appeared to represent a strong influence in the contemporary history sector of the History Institute—continued to show considerable scholarly objectivity despite the hardening of the official line and showed a notable laggardness in keeping abreast of the ideological demands of the times. In the following paragraphs this relatively objective trend in Soviet postwar historiography will be examined.

An example of this style of scholarship was an article entitled "The Formation of the Bloc of Fascist Aggressors," by P. Osipova, which appeared in *Questions of History* in 1947.[8] It presented a detailed, virtually nonideological exposition of international events in the prewar years, describing the motivations and policies of the democratic and Axis powers alike almost solely in terms of national self-interest. There were only two or three places where the role of the Soviet Union was mentioned, almost in passing, and the author's praise of Soviet actions on these occasions hardly exceeded the limits of pardonable *parti pris*. All the obvious openings for moralizations or ideological sermons that the narrative presented were passed over. At times, the author even took pains to blunt the ideological edge of the events described. Regarding the anti-Comintern pact, for example, it was said: "As the years immediately following the agreement showed, the so-called anti-Comintern pact was directed not only against the Soviet Union but also against such states as France, England, etc."[9] The Munich pact was dismissed in a line or two, and although it was called "shameful," there was no mention of ulterior Western motives in connection with it.[10] The U.S. was virtually not mentioned, and nowhere pejoratively, in the article.

During this period, a number of articles of a fairly objective nature on the origins of the Pacific war appeared. Professor G. Deborin, in the subsequent issue of *Questions of History,* discussed the Pearl Harbor attack within a clearly defined ideological framework, yet in a way that was not unsympathetic to the U.S. His quoting of Hull and Roosevelt, for example, had the effect of personalizing and humanizing the American experience and the American leaders and seemed intended to call forth the reader's sympathy for the sentiments expressed.[11]

A year later, a much more detached and scholarly article on the origins of the Pacific war, "From the History of Japanese-American Conversations in 1941," appeared from the pen of B. Rodov.[12] This was a careful reconstruction of diplomatic events during the final weeks before the war, based largely on the hearings before the Joint Congressional Committee on the investigation of the Pearl Harbor attack. There was not a single really derogatory word about the U.S. in the article, or even a typical Communist formula. Unlike the official propaganda, which always sought to build up the significance of the Soviet Union in the calculations of foreign statesmen, Rodov interpreted Japanese policy as having been directed solely against the U.S. and failed to mention hostility toward the U.S.S.R. as a spring of Japanese policy. At one place, he produced a quotation from the Tanaka memorial—"If we wish to control China, we must first of all crush the United States"[13]—which, in its effect, ran directly counter to the official line, i.e., that the Soviet Union was the major obstacle to Japanese expansion and the major preoccupation of its leaders. All in all, this article was a remarkably detached and objective piece of historical writing. Later in the year, Rodov appeared in print again, with essentially the same point of view. This time, in a review of *Pearl Harbor, The Story of the Secret War* (New York, 1947) by the American author G. Morgenstern, Rodov defended Roosevelt against the charge that he had provoked the Pacific war. In his article, Rodov repeatedly invoked the "official American documentation," or the "official documentation that fully confirms," with apparent full confidence in the reliability of these sources.[14]

A number of more substantial historical works that appeared during this period also revealed considerable objectivity, or at least minimal ideological distortion. V. Avarin's *Struggle for the Pacific Ocean: Japanese-American Contradictions* was such a book.[15] It had a tendentious thesis—that the strategic situation of the Soviet Union, and the operations of the Red Army in Europe, exerted a continuing decisive influence on the course of events in the Pacific—but, apart from this, it was a creditable Soviet effort to give a coherent account of the Pacific war. It displayed only a patina of Communist historical devices (at least in the chapters devoted to the war itself), and, on the whole, interpreted the policies of the contending states in terms of straight power politics and national self-interest. A general sympathy for the Allies was apparent. While Avarin attributed the Japanese capitulation mainly to the Soviet entry into the war, he did not deprecate the toll of the Allied air attacks and acknowledged the "definite" effect of the first atomic bomb.

A characteristic feature of Avarin's style was his tendency to depart from the lexicon of Soviet political analysis to introduce data or observations that tended to contradict, or at least muddy, the general ideological premises that he professed. His acknowledgment of the great help shown the American troops by the Philippine partisans, for example, tended to refute his proposition that the colonial policies of the Allies had deprived them of human resources. His comments on the American cabinet of 1940 virtually threw into the discard the Communist stereotype of American political reality. Consider, for example, his following words.

Into the new government, on July 21, entered the Republicans Stimson as Secretary of War and Knox as Secretary of the Navy. The American press noted that the new ministers were adherents of a "decisive policy" and wished to help England "by all means." The memory of the diplomatic measures applied by Stimson in connection with the seizure of Manchuria by Japan, in the years when he was Secretary of State, was still fresh in American minds. . . . Knox had participated in the Spanish-American War in the volunteer cavalry of T. Roosevelt, and, as a major, had taken part in World War I. He and Stimson were representatives of those circles of the Republican Party that stood for a speedy militarization of the country, for a policy of the "strong hand" in foreign relations, and for the most active participation of the U.S.A. in international affairs.[16]

Avarin also remarked in this connection that Franklin Roosevelt resembled Theodore Roosevelt—"his kinsman and political teacher"—a most unorthodox comparison, which seemed to admit the "imperialist" American President into the select circle of Soviet-approved bourgeois figures.

Avarin's attitude toward the Chinese National Government, and Chiang Kai-shek personally, was remarkably friendly. He complained of the obstructionist activities of "reactionary circles" within the Kuomintang and of the hostile acts of "Kuomintang generals" against the Communist 8th Army, but he did not include Chiang Kai-shek, or the National government as a whole, in these charges. In several places, he spoke of the war aims of the Chinese Government in favorable terms, quoting the original texts without qualifying commentary. For example, regarding the Cairo conference, he said the following:

In Cairo, November 22–26, a conference of the heads of the three states, England, the U.S.A., and China, took place. On December 1, a declaration was published in the name of Roosevelt, Churchill, and Chiang Kai-shek, which proclaimed the basic principles of the territorial changes that would take place in the Pacific Ocean area after the victory over Japan. According to these principles, the three allies "do not desire any acquisitions for themselves and have no thoughts of territorial expansion. Their aim is to deprive Japan of all islands in the Pacific Ocean it had occupied since the beginning of World War I in 1914, and to return to China all territory that Japan had torn away, such as Manchuria, Formosa, and the Pescadores."[17]

The cloudiness of Soviet policy toward China in the postwar period makes it difficult to determine whether, or to what degree, Avarin's attitude toward the Chinese was more friendly than the official mood of the time. Max Beloff, in his heavily documented book *Soviet Policy in the Far East, 1944–1951,* says that the Soviet attitude toward the National Government had hardened as early as 1946, and that, although Chiang Kai-shek continued to be treated with forbearance, from that time on the Chinese Government was no longer referred to as the "National" Government but as the "Kuomintang" Government.[18] Avarin, however, repeatedly used the term "National China" and referred to its government simply as the "Chinese Government." It seems safe to say that Avarin at least skirted the outer limits of that amicability toward China that the Soviet Government tolerated during the period of its own uncertainty in this policy sphere.

Avarin's account of the Japanese capitulation went as far in acknowledging the role of the Allies in this event as any Soviet account could go. This is what he said:

Japan suffered increasingly great damage from the air bombardment of the Allies. In particular, the first atomic bomb dropped by American aviation on August 5 [*sic*] on the port of Hiroshima produced a definite effect. The second atomic bomb was dropped August 9 on the port of Nagasaki. However, the Japanese state leaders took great consolation from the fact that they did not anticipate early decisive operations by the Allies. The Allies put off these operations until much larger forces could be concentrated against Japan. The Japanese imperialists also found consolation in the military and political situation in China, which has been described above. They prepared themselves for a long and bitter struggle against England, the U.S.A., and China, hoping that changes in the international political situation still might save them from final defeat. . . .

Two weeks after the publication of the Potsdam declaration, a new great historical event took place that placed an end to all the plans of the Japanese imperialists who counted on prolonging the war. On

August 8, 1945, the Soviet Government announced that from August 9 it would consider itself in a state of war with Japan.[19]

Commentary is hardly necessary, but it may be useful to point out that even in such small details as the description of Hiroshima and Nagasaki as ports, i.e., as military targets, this account leans as far as possible, under Soviet conditions, toward a fair appraisal of the Allied operations.

The relative objectivity of this book was brought out in a dramatic way by a second book that Avarin published, under obvious political pressure, in 1952.[20] This second book had the same title as the earlier one, but a new subtitle: "Aggression of the U.S.A. and England, Their Contradictions, and the Freedom Struggle of the Peoples." The almost complete reversal of Avarin's views in this edition was partially concealed by the fiction that the second volume was a new book rather than a revision of the old. In the foreword, the author wrote: "While working on this book, the author has striven to the greatest extent to take into account the critical observations that were expressed in the press and in the discussion in the Academy of Social Sciences regarding another of his books, *Struggle for the Pacific Ocean: Japanese-American Contradictions.*" In fact, the second book was a completely rewritten and recast account of the Pacific war. In contrast to the generally objective stance of the first, it was virtually apoplectic in its denunciation of the U.S. Even the literary style was unrecognizable as that of the same author. Citation mania was reduced to the absurdity of quoting Stalin to support the factual statement that Germany attacked the Anglo-Franco-American bloc before launching its invasion of the Soviet Union. The Allies were given no credit for winning the Pacific war, and the atomic bomb was mentioned only in the context of an argument against its significance in this event.[21]

Another postwar work that, in some respects, was even less affected by ideological preconceptions than Avarin's first book was V. Lan's *The U.S.A. from the First to the Second World War*.[22] The book was, of course, written from a Soviet, even a Communist viewpoint, but it lacked the familiar trappings of Soviet historiography, such as the usual foreword expounding the doctrine of imperialist crisis, etc. What is more surprising, it was almost a compendium of essentially favorable information about the U.S., e.g., that "not only millionaires, but millions of ordinary Americans could find refuge from the severe winter under the warm rays of the Florida sun,"[23] or that in the state of Vermont "there is hardly a family without a savings book,"[24] etc. Regarding the prehistory of the war, which it touched only tangentially, it gave a similarly nonideological account of American policy.

The last chapter, which came closest to the subject of this study, was focused on the efforts of the U.S. Government to prepare the country for war. A large section was devoted to the debate over neutrality legislation, which was described in terms of internationalist vs. isolationist pressures, without any overtones of class analysis. At one point, Lan spoke of the desire of the "Cliveden Set" and "anti-Soviet circles" in France and the U.S. to direct Hitlerite aggression eastward, but he took pains to dilute his mild criticism of U.S. policy in this connection. Quoting Professor Beard to the effect that Roosevelt, together with Chamberlain and Daladier, was morally responsible for Munich, Lan said:

This venerable American historian, criticizing the foreign policy of Roosevelt not impartially, expresses himself too sharply in the present case. But the fact that two or three days before the signing of the agreement, on September 26 and 27, the President of the U.S.A. twice requested Hitler to continue negotiations with the aim of preserving peace, created the impression in the country that America had also contributed its mite to Munich.[25]

Lan also demonstrated his independence in his rejection of the rigid stylization of Soviet political exposition. His style reflected a spirit of contingency, an un-Marxian appreciation of the tentativeness of historical events. A final quotation, taken from the summary of the discussion of the neutrality debate, may convey something of this flavor of his book:

It was the summer of 1939. The discussion was in full swing. Many in the U.S.A. defended peace in words. All the disputants spoke about identical aims. They divided only over the means [proposed] and the prognoses. Who was right: the Government or the Congress, the majority or the minority in Congress?

The answer was not long in coming. The summer of 1939 was drawing to its close. The pages of history turned quickly.[26]

Another work that holds considerable interest from the standpoint of this investigation was the first volume of a series publication entitled *Works on Modern and Contemporary History,* which was brought out by the History Institute in 1948.[27] This volume was severely criticized later for many departures from ideological orthodoxy. Most of the articles contained in it fall somewhat outside our purview, but one, "The German-Fascist *Drang nach Osten* after Munich," by F. I. Notovich, is clearly within our field of interest. This was a scholarly piece of work, which, although it expressed a moral indignation against the men of Munich, was practically free of ideological verbiage. The main criticism later directed against this article was that it described the Munich agreement as a "capitulation" rather than as a "deal" or "bargain." The text supports this criticism fully.

In one or two passages, Notovich spoke of Western diplomacy as being predicated on an eventual clash between Germany and Russia. Ironically, this conception was expressed most clearly in a quotation from Keynes, which was given in a footnote.[23] The few scattered statements of this kind, however, were clearly overshadowed by the author's basic conception, which was that at Munich and subsequently, Western policy was capitulationist. The article began with the words "The Munich capitulation," a phrase repeated throughout.

The author's lack of sympathy for the official interpretation of Munich as a "deal" (the article was published after the appearance of *Falsificators of History*) was indicated in several places where he raised the question of Western motives in connection with the Munich agreement and refrained from giving a definitive answer. At one point, for example, speaking about the hope of the men of Munich that their policy would lead to peace, he inserted the inconclusive parenthetical remark "sincerely or hypocritically" after the word "hope," without qualifying it in any other way.[29] Later, he expressed his dubiety even more clearly. Speaking about the Franco-German declaration of mutual consultation after Munich, he said: "Whether there was an agreement between Ribbentrop and Bonnet that, in exchange for a formal recognition by Germany of the French eastern border as 'final,' gave [Germany] complete freedom of action in eastern and southeastern Europe . . . remains unclear on the basis of present documentation."[30] His subsequent account of the *démarches* of France against continued German expansionist activities in eastern Europe indicated that he himself did not believe that such an agreement had taken place.

There were a number of other distinctive features of the Notovich article. For example, it was devoid of the usual references to Marxist authorities. Although the fifty-page text carried extensive scholarly annotations, only two or three references to Soviet sources appeared. Also, references to anti-Semitism within Germany were unusually frequent.

Several other works and authors deserve mention here, although the evidence linking them with the trend under investigation is not as conclusive as that considered above. Perhaps the most interesting of these was a book published in 1947, by Professor G. Deborin, entitled *International Relations and the Foreign Policy of the U.S.S.R., 1917–1945,* Volume IV: *The Years of the Great Patriotic War.*[31] This book was apparently withdrawn from circulation sometime in 1949 and is not now available, so that our knowledge of it is limited to the critical information provided on it by the Soviet press. According to this information, the book was published by the Higher Diplomatic School as an informal student manual ("according to the rules for manuscripts") and enjoyed circulation in educational institutions in this capacity. Apparently, official attention was drawn to the book when the contemporary history sector of the History Institute attempted to republish it under the seal of the Academy of Sciences.

The substantive criticism of the book was focused on its alleged pro-American bias. It was said that the book presented U.S. foreign policy during World War II "just as American imperialists themselves attempt to portray it." This interpretation, it was said, conveyed the impression that the U.S. Government was opposed to the anti-Soviet policies of Churchill and the American imperialists, and that it was a staunch friend of the Soviet Union throughout the struggle. Thus the book concealed the "struggle within the anti-Hitler coalition" during the war and ignored the "fundamental opposition between the foreign policy of the U.S.S.R., on the one hand, and of the U.S.A. and Great Britain, on the other." On a more specific issue, the second front, the book also was said to have given a distorted interpretation. The Western delay in opening a second front was attributed to the inability of "shortsighted" U.S. and British leaders to evaluate the developing situation in 1942 correctly and to their overestimation of the Hitler forces. Finally, the official critics hinted darkly at improper motives in the publication of the book.

It is generally known that editions published "according to the rules for manuscripts" are, as a rule, published in dozens, or hundreds, of copies. Such is not the case with Professor Deborin's book; it has been published in 9,000 copies. Some of our scientific organizations publish immature and tainted books in mass editions "under the rules for manuscripts." It is necessary to put an end to such incorrect, antistate practices in literature publishing.[32]

Certainly, these remarks cover a broad gamut of ideological sins, and there can be little doubt that this book was quite out of harmony with the official spirit of the times. We must be cautious, however, about accepting the Soviet criticism of 1949 at its face value. On the evidence, we cannot say Deborin's book was more liberal or more friendly to the U.S. than other works that appeared in the early postwar period, such as those considered above. But we may infer with reasonable certainty that the book was much softer than the post-1947 line. The feature of the episode that presumably agitated the official critics was not so much the unorthodoxy of the book as the unorthodoxy of the contemporary history sector of the History Institute in attempting to republish the book in 1949. The identity of the editor of the proposed new edition, Professor L. I. Zubok, may also have had something to do with the ferocity of the official attack.

L. I. Zubok was the History Institute's most prominent expert on American history and published frequently on this subject during the postwar period. Most of his work dealt with inter-American relations and thus falls outside the scope of our survey. Since Zubok was severely attacked at that time, however, for showing a pro-American attitude, it will be useful to review some of his work very briefly, so that we may better understand his position and the nature of the official historical reaction. In 1946, Zubok published an article on American-Mexican relations that provided a nonpolemic account of U.S. foreign policy in that area.[33] In the following year, he dealt with the history of U.S. policy in Cuba in a somewhat more doctrinaire way.[34] This article was certainly not friendly to the U.S., but, on the other hand, it was not a propaganda broadside. Despite the obvious openings the story gave him (the history of the Platt Amendment), Zubok did not embellish the account excessively with ideological moralizations. In 1948, he contributed an article on U.S. policy in Haiti to the first volume of *Works on Modern and Contemporary History*.[35] This article was much in the style of his article on Cuba, and similarly contained a cautiously worded appraisal of the "good-neighbor policy." The substance of Zubok's appraisal was that U.S. domination had been so firmly established in Latin America by the 1930's that strong-arm methods of control were no longer necessary. He conveyed the impression, however, that Roosevelt's policy constituted a watershed in U.S.–Latin American relations. Finally, Zubok edited a volume entitled *Contemporary History,* which was published as a textbook for the higher Party schools in 1948.[36] This book was thoroughly impregnated with a Marxist outlook, and deserves mention here only because of one or two incautious statements it contained. In one place, Zubok said: "In relation to Hitlerite Germany, Roosevelt from the very beginning took a definite position, coming out against fascist aggression."[37] In another: "The government of Roosevelt wished to reconcile itself neither with the aggression of Germany in Europe nor the aggression of Japan in the Far East."[38] These statements, in the opinion of later critics, showed American policy in much too favorable a light and specifically seemed to exonerate it from any responsibility for the encouragement of Hitler's aggression.

Taken together, the evidence described above does not explain why Zubok should have been treated so severely by the critics in 1949. It is probable that, as an expert on American history, he was, ex officio as it were, tainted with a kind of guilt by association. This could have been particularly important at the time, since in the reaction against the Varga school even the most innocent acknowledgments of good in America (and Zubok made such acknowledgments with respect to Roosevelt) could be construed as an argument in favor of the "exceptional" nature of American capitalism. Indeed, the Deborin book, which Zubok edited, was charged with just such a crime. Not only would his professional association with America have made him suspect in the eyes of critics, but it would also have made him a particularly suitable victim for an object lesson on the dangers of undue interest in America.

As the critics were clear to point out, historians were held responsible not only for what they published but also for what they said. A statement made in a classroom lecture illustrates the relatively objective trend in Soviet postwar historical analysis. The case in point was that of Professor Zvavich, a man whose name was often linked with Zubok's in the official criticisms. He was quoted as having made the following startling statement: "In the lecture course given at the Higher Diplomatic School, Zvavich committed a direct falsification of history, asserting that a turning point in the course of the war took place as a result of the landing of the Americans in Italy."[39]

Again, as with Zubok, it is difficult to evaluate the official criticism. Quite probably, Zvavich's difficulties, like those of Zubok, arose not from any undue admiration for the West (his field was modern British history), but from the unavoidable political pitfalls facing anyone who attempted to interpret the Western democracies to a Soviet audience at that time.

Summing up this review of the relatively objective trend in Soviet postwar historiography, we might say that Soviet historians gave evidence of a capacity and willingness to deal with the Western role in the war in a reasonably objective way as long as they were given free editorial rein to do so. This leads to the assumption that the historians' subsequent acceptance of the Party line on the war was a *pis aller* not carrying with it any genuine acceptance of political expedience as the criterion of historical truth.

The Tightening of the Official Line and the Historians' Reaction

While these relatively scholarly works were appearing, the ideological reaction was taking firm hold in the historical community. At first, it manifested itself in relatively obscure forms—in reports, book reviews, etc.—and then in a stream of narrowly ideological articles that, by the end of 1947, had become a flood. By that time,

too, the last strongholds of scholarly urbanity in the editorial
policy of *Questions of History* had fallen. The section of the journal
devoted to a bibliography of historical works published abroad,
which for some time after the war had provided Soviet historians
with a tenuous link to the world community, was discontinued in
mid-1947. It had provided a broad listing of Western documentary
publications, memoir material, and books dealing with the national
war efforts of the democracies, selected without any noticeable
ideological bias. Titles such as *The Persecutions of the Catholic
Church in Poland: Reports presented by H.E. Cardinal Hlond,
Primate of Poland, to Pope Pius XII. Vatican broadcasts and other
reliable evidence. Preface by H.E. A. Cardinal Hinsley*. (London,
1941) were not unusual.[40] A somewhat similar fate befell the
"Historical Science Abroad" section of *Voprosy Istorii*. Throughout the early postwar period, this section had always been distinguished by the utmost objectivity and scientific detachment. It
carried news items on historical activities throughout the world, information on foreign library accessions, appreciative obituaries
when the occasion required, etc. The first sign of ideological bias
in this section appeared in the fall of 1947, when a reference to the
"academic lackeys of American imperialism" was made in a report
on the previous annual meeting of the American Historical Association.[41] Beginning with the next issue, news from the U.S. ceased
to be the first item in this section, as it generally had been until
then. Starting with the first issue of 1948, the title of this section
was changed from "Historical Science Abroad" to "Abroad," as
if to proclaim the Soviet view that the dignity of science could be
claimed only by Marxist-Leninists.

The full fury of the ideological reaction fell on the historical
community during the years 1948 and 1949, when, under the
goad of the Party press,* a series of meetings was held to place

* The first of the important critical articles appears to have been N.
Yakovlev, "O prepodavanii otechestvennoy istorii," *Bolshevik*, No. 22
(1947). It is worth noting, in this connection, that there was no independent

one historian after another on the rack of public criticism for the edification of his fellows. While at first these meetings displayed some restraint and decorum, as time went on they degenerated into carnivals of denunciation. The climax of this campaign came in the spring of 1949, when the second issue of *Questions of History* for that year was held up for five months while a reorganization of the editorial board was effected. In the following 1949 issues a series of directive articles appeared laying down strict guidelines for historians to follow in the future. Thenceforth, until after Stalin's death, virtually all life appeared to have been snuffed out of the historical community.

In examining the nature of the historians' reaction to this ideological campaign, we will see whether, in their deportment before the ideological firing squads, they displayed any allegiance to those standards of historical honesty (or disdain for the political principles substituted for these standards) that, on the basis of some of their earlier postwar writings, might have been expected of them.

To begin with, there were signs that the historians attempted to deflect or blunt or even shield each other from the sharp edge of Party criticism. The behavior of the editorial board of *Questions of History* itself was remarkable in this respect. For example, in the case of N. Rubinshteyn, the first victim of the ideological reaction, the board displayed tact and forbearance by allowing him to initiate the discussion of his criticized textbook rather than subjecting him to immediate attack by others.[42] Its action in the case of I. I. Mints was even bolder. At a time when Mints had become the main target of Party attacks, the editorial board allowed him to publish a lead article in the first issue of 1949, which, in effect, con-

---

reaction in the historical community either to the 1946 Party decree on literature or to the 1947 discussion of Aleksandrov's textbook on the history of West European philosophy, although the relevance of the latter event to history was frequently emphasized in subsequent criticisms.

stituted an apologia for the historical community.[43] This article
listed all the names of the leading Soviet historians, proclaimed
their contributions to Soviet historical science, and (perhaps by a
slip of the pen, because the rest of his article was very dutiful in
this respect) attributed to his own colleagues, rather than to
Stalin, the credit for laying the "basis for the study of the Soviet
period of the history of our country."[44] That both of these interven-
tions by *Questions of History* in the Party's disciplinary process
were deliberate was indicated in later criticisms.[45]

In addition to *Questions of History* itself, individual historians
also made efforts to stem the course of party reaction. At the beginning of the critical campaign, for example, there was at least one
historian (K. Vazilevich) who stood openly against the basic
chauvinist tendency of the official line. "We are not inclined to
grovel before the West," he said. "We carry our culture with dignity. . . . But to tear off the history of Russia from the history
of other countries—this would mean to return to a past that has
been condemned, and it would hardly be right to start off on such
a path."[46] In the first discussion of Mints's book, it was reported
that one speaker (A. I. Gukovskiy) attempted to impugn Mints's
loyalty. All the subsequent speakers, it was noted, "unanimously
rejected" this insinuation.[47] Again, in the discussion of *Works on
Modern and Contemporary History,* it was reported: "Attempts to
soften the sharpness of the criticism appeared, for example, in the
speech of A. Z. Manfred, who accompanied his acknowledgment
of the mistaken character of Eggerts' article with ambiguous com-
pliments regarding the author's 'great skill,' 'ability to master the
material,' etc."[48]

Not infrequently, individual authors showed considerable stubbornness in refusing to bow meekly to official criticism. I. M.
Lemin, for example, the author of *The Foreign Policy of Great
Britain from Versailles to Locarno,* was reported sticking to his
guns at the end of the critical session on his book.

It is necessary to note, at the same time, the unserious and irresponsible attitude the author of the book himself displayed toward the discussion. Admitting, in general terms, that "certainly there are many shortcomings in the book," that "there are certain bad-sounding words," and that "the tone is inappropriate in a number of cases," I. M. Lemin at the same time attempted, without any proof, to deny all the concrete and argued complaints and observations about the book made by the speakers. As a result of the false position taken by him, I. M. Lemin in fact rejected the critical review of his book [and] the criticism to which it was subjected at the discussion, and his concluding words failed completely to satisfy those present.[49]

The cynical remarks some historians made during these critical sessions revealed, more eloquently than any disquisition, their full awareness of the purely political considerations that motivated the official reaction. The complaint by a Soviet economist on another occasion that he had been criticized by the *"plat du jour* method" seemed to characterize the attitude of a number of historians toward the campaign. For example, Professor Lutskiy, in attempting to ward off attacks on his sector of the History Institute, referred to what he called a commonly held opinion in historical circles "that the history of Soviet society is not history, but current politics."[50] A similar theme in the defensive remarks of the criticized historians was the complaint that they had been victimized by the swift change in the official line after the war. For example, A. I. Andreyev, the author of an article on the visit of Peter the Great to England, employed this defense.

A. I. Andreyev attempted to justify his incorrect and harmful position in this question by the fact that he wrote the article in 1942, for the jubilee of Newton. At that time, it appeared to him appropriate to emphasize the role of England in the reforming activity of Peter the Great. If he wrote this article now, said A. I. Andreyev, he certainly would not commit the mistake for which he is being blamed.[51]

F. I. Notovich, the author of the article "The German-Fascist *Drang nach Osten* after Munich," used the same defense.

Still more unsatisfactory was the speech of F. I. Notovich, who at first refused to recognize any substantial mistakes at all in his understanding or evaluation of the Munich policy in his article. Only in his second speech, which followed the decisive criticism of his first, did Comrade Notovich acknowledge that he had permitted "false notes" in it and that his article did not correspond to the demands of militant Party historical science. However, even in his second speech, F. I. Notovich insinuated false notes. He explained the errors of his article not as arising from a misunderstanding of the essence of the Munich agreement, but as a result of the fact that he had "printed in 1948 an article written in 1945."[52]

Perhaps more significant than these displays of individual courage or stubbornness were the signs (naturally heavily veiled in Soviet sources) of something like an organized resistance by the historical community to the Party's ideological campaign. This appeared most clearly in the virtual boycott of the discussion of Rubinshteyn's textbook held by the Ministry of Higher Education, in March, 1948. Of the speakers reported at the meeting, only three appeared to be historians of importance (S. A. Pokrovskiy, A. L. Sidorov, and Ye. N. Gorodetskiy); the others were mainly docents, or professors from outside Moscow. The absence of the first-rate historical figures from the meeting was all the more striking in view of the high sponsorship of the affair and the importance the authorities obviously attached to it. At the meeting, both Sidorov and Gorodetskiy referred to the absence of the major professors in terms suggesting that a "feat of silence" was being performed. Complaining that the initiative for the criticism had come from outside the historical community, Sidorov stated: "Even now, at this present conference, the majority of the members of the department [of Moscow State University] are absent. . . . A certain inwardness on the part of these institutions [the History Institute and the Academy of Social Sciences], and the absence of prominent historians at the present meeting, characterize, to a significant degree, the general position on the historical front."[53] Gorodetskiy referred sarcastically to the "absence of the so-called pillars of historical science from the discussion."[54] Later, on several occasions, it was implied that this absence of the Moscow historical community from the meeting had been a deliberate act.[55]

Later criticism revealed other cases of group opposition to the Party's ideological campaign. At the end of 1948, a lead article in *Questions of History* asserted: "There were cases when the criticism of mistakes [recently made in the press, etc.] was met with hostility in the Institute."[56] Also: "The Institute did not organize work on the exposure of foreign bourgeois historiography and did not conduct an attack on foreign falsificators of history. This work, until recently, has been considered in the Institute as 'outside the plan,' and the workers of the Institute shunned it."[57]

This last remark provides a fitting epilogue to this review of the historians' reaction to the Party's Cold War demands on the historical community. As the evidence presented above clearly indicates, many historians had indeed "shunned it" as long as possible. Attitudes toward particular aspects or consequences of the Party's demands were not distinguishable. The resistance which the historians displayed was evoked not by clashes over particular issues but by professional disdain for the political criteria that defined the Party's demands. The most striking feature of this performance was the indisputable evidence it provided that the historians understood the nature of the capitulations they were forced to make.

Thus we see that the professional historians were blocked off from the military history of the war by political decisions taken at the war's end and thenceforth restricted themselves to the diplomatic history of the wartime period. In this field, a significant number of them displayed a relatively objective attitude toward the

West up through 1947, and some even beyond that date. This seemed to reflect the influence of professional standards rather than any emotional or political attraction toward the West. However, when the Party's ideological assault on the West began to affect the historical community, some historians did resist it and also showed disdain for the cogency and relevance of the political considerations motivating it.

5

The Writers and the War

One other important segment of Soviet society—the literary community—made its contribution to the history of the war and recorded its attitudes toward the official version of that history. During the course of the war, more than 900 writers were engaged in serving the needs of the war-enlarged propaganda effort. As troubadors of the national epic, their words naturally reflected the political ends they were called to serve; but their reportorial talents and the boldness and independence that they, as a group, had begun to reacquire during the war lent some of their writings a vividness that distinguished them from the bulk of official reportage. By virtue of these same qualities, the writers' attitude toward the postwar propaganda on the war demonstrated a more tenacious opposition to the official varnishing of reality than that shown by other groups.

This chapter will set forth examples from the wartime and immediate postwar literature illustrating how writers, by handling approved themes in fresh and original ways, managed to convey truths about the war that were not shown in other media. It will also consider examples of the open opposition shown by some of the writers to the version of the war encouraged by official propaganda.

REALISTIC PAGES FROM WARTIME LITERATURE

Soviet wartime literature diverged most noticeably from the style of later propaganda in its treatment of problems affecting civic and military behavior during the war. The greater realism it displayed in this sphere was partly the result of the conscious policy of the government, which had found, during the emergency, that nonsocialist values such as national patriotism could inspire the Soviet man with martial virtues his "socialist make-up" had failed to provide; in part, it flowed from the general lightening of the weight of political self-consciousness among writers during the war, which permitted them some freedom to record their observations without constant thought of critical reprisals. Consequently, in this literature, there could sometimes be found portrayals of loyalty and disloyalty, of courage and cowardice, of initiative and mistakes, having the stamp of direct observation and the ring of truth.

Simonov's *Days and Nights,* one of the best known of the wartime novels, had some of these positive qualities.[1] Despite its slickness and political stylization, it contained glimmers of truth. The theme of the novel was the indomitable courage of the ordinary Russian soldier. The source of this courage, as Simonov portrayed it, was the devotion of the Russian to his native land. This was not necessarily a political phenomenon. One of the characters in the novel, a veteran of World War I, whose manner and speech betrayed the style of a Czarist soldier, symbolized the continuity of national patriotism embodied in the two great Russian wars against Germany. It was Simonov's intention to emphasize that all Russians, regardless of past attachments, were bound together in the fellowship of national devotion. This was brought out also in connection with the one negative character of the novel, a traitor spy, the son of an Orthodox priest. Instead of denouncing the clerical background of this spy as the reason for his treachery,

Simonov took care to emphasize the simple national loyalty of the priest-father: "He never raised his hand for or against power, because everything around him was Russia, and so power over it stayed Russian."[2]

A similarly nonpolitical interpretation of the sources of military loyalty was given by Grossman in his wartime stories and reportage. Unlike Simonov, however, he did not emphasize the abstract qualities of national patriotism as much as the personal attachments of soldiers for their buddies, their *esprit de corps*, as a basic motivation of their behavior. His remarks regarding the Siberian division at Stalingrad were typical:

One cannot help wondering how this magnificent stubbornness was forged. It was, of course, compounded of both national character and the realization of a great responsibility, of both rugged Siberian obstinacy and splendid military and political schooling and stern discipline. But I want to mention one other trait that played no little part in this grand and tragic epic—the astonishing morale, the firm attachment that knit together the men of the Siberian Division, and the spirit of Spartan modesty typical of the commanders of this Division.[3]

In another place, Grossman analyzes the sources of military courage. While admitting that a sense of duty, hatred for the enemy, and desire for revenge played a part, he gave greater prominence to such nonpolitical motives as: the conviction that one would not be killed, the conviction that one would be killed and hence the futility of caution, the "oblivion that comes to a man in battle."[4]

The relative realism of the wartime literature was reinforced by occasional snatches of rough and callous soldiers' humor. This comic relief stood in stark contrast to the politically conscious stodginess of official pronouncements on the character and motivation of Soviet soldiers in war. Grossman, for example, described an air alert in which momentary uncertainty as to the nationality of the approaching planes was resolved by the determination that they were Russian. "They're ours, alright," he has someone say. "Where's my helmet?"[5] In another place, he records a soldier's mock advice called out to a German battery firing on the dugout of his chief of artillery: "Two yards to the right. Now a yard to the left. Bulls-eye. Hold it!"[6] The fact that this harmless anecdote was changed in the 1946 edition of Grossman's work to make the last phrase read: "Hey, Chief, look out!"[7] highlights the sensitive and humorless mood of Soviet censorship, and helps to explain why humor was extremely rare in Soviet accounts of the war.

The wartime literature sometimes spoke with surprising candor about the negative phenomena of war, such as cowardice, desertion, collaboration with the enemy. Vershigora, for example, in his *Men With a Clear Conscience,* described how, in his first battle action, he ordered Russian soldiers who were surrendering to the Germans to be mowed down together with their captors.[8] In the same place, he spoke of a German tommy-gunner "firing at a whole platoon of backs."[9] Perhaps the most common of the negative themes in the wartime literature, although seldom mentioned directly, was the phenomenon of collaboration. A strikingly unveiled account of this phenomenon, in its sensitiveness and depth of perception perhaps unmatched in Soviet literature, appeared in Grossman's story "The Old Schoolmaster."

That night, the little town gasped in the clutches of all that was shady and wicked, evil and filthy, of all that wakened and stirred, roused by the arrival of the Hitlerites and stretching forth to meet them. Out of their holes and cellars crawled traitors; the weak in spirit tore up their volumes of Lenin, their Party membership cards and letters and burned them, tore the pictures of their brothers down from the walls. In their abject souls fawning words of disavowal matured; thoughts of vengeance for some silly quarrel in the market were born, for some chance word hastily spoken; hearts filled with hardness, selfishness, and indifference. Cowards, fearing for their own safety, concocted reports against their neighbors in order to save their own skins. And so it was and so it had been in all big and little cities of big and little states—

wherever the Hitlerites set foot, the turbid dregs rose from the bottoms of rivers and lakes, toads swam to the surface; thistles sprang up where wheat had grown.[10]

In the same story, Grossman made one of the rare references in Soviet literature to the *Nationale Freiwilligen Bataillone,* the Russian volunteer contingents of the German Army.[11]

The wartime literature also contained hints of the chaos caused by the German invasion and the ineptness of the Soviet Army during the early part of the war. Hints of military confusion, of panic in the towns, were scattered in the early pages of Vershigora's book. Simonov made similar hints and—what is more surprising—added to them a reproachful account of the early retreats that verged on an open criticism of Soviet strategy. Consider, for example, these words of his principal character:

Millions of cubic meters of dirt have been dug up from the frontier all the way to here, and all for nothing. Why? Because we so often dig a line behind ourselves but then don't place soldiers in it in advance, or don't give them guns, or machine guns—give them nothing to fight with. And the Germans, once they outflank us, get to these lines before we do. And there go the fortifications, time after time. Meanwhile, we retreat to the town, stand with our backs to it, and dig new trenches—not in three months, but in three days, which is all we actually have, and we have to fight them to the end, to the death.[12]

These glimmers of realism in wartime literature provide insights into the broader problem of the attitudes of the writers toward the propaganda version of the war. They suggest the difficulty writers felt in compressing political purposes into artistic forms, the difficulty of erasing from a work with literary pretensions all traces of realism that might be distasteful to the sensibilities of political superiors. They suggest that, however well motivated a writer might be, he could not but run afoul of the inherent contradiction between reality as politically idealized and reality as observed. This tension between the discipline of politics and the internal discipline of literature caused a number of writers in the postwar period to voice their open opposition to the trend of official propaganda on the war.

THE POLEMIC OF PANFEROV

The most dramatic episode in the postwar collision between propaganda policy on the interpretation of the war and the eye-witness testimony of the writers was the article "Crocks and Potsherds," which appeared in the literary journal *October,* in 1946, from the pen of its editor, F. Panferov.[13] Panferov's article was a plaintive and bitter denunciation of the literary bureaucracy (and inescapably, though implicitly, of the political powers supporting it) for promoting a false, prettified version of the sufferings, terrors, and majestic achievements of the war. In its range of indictment and passion of advocacy, the article was a classic expression of the postwar open opposition that flickered against the official line on the war.

The occasion for Panferov's article was a relatively insignificant dispute between *October* and *Literary Gazette* over the literary merits of the novel *Flaming Land* (*Ognennaya Zemlya*) by Arkadiy Perventsev. The dispute over the novel, which dealt with the Soviet landing on the Kerch Peninsula, began with a critical review in *Literary Gazette,* by A. Erlikh. The criticism was not particularly harsh and was of a literary nature: "The last line, the last word of the novel has been read. . . . The book is closed. Almost immediately, the episodes, the scenes, the characterizations, conceived without creative inspiration, are forgotten."[14] Some months later, *October* responded with its own favorable evaluation of the novel, and Erlikh was specifically disputed.[15] This was followed up by Panferov's own article, which, in addition to the broad-ranging denunciation of the literary bureaucracy mentioned above, contained a bitter personal attack on Erlikh. The sequel followed quickly, with a venomous personal criticism of Panferov in the *Literary Gazette* of June 22, 1946, and an official rebuke in *Pravda* two days later. By this time, the issue had shifted from the literary merits of *Flaming Land* to the political question of the official interpretation of the war.

The substance of Panferov's article was the complaint that the critics (and again it must be assumed that Panferov understood the articles of the critics to be litmus-paper recordings of the trends of political opinion) opposed any honest portrayal of the war that conveyed a true measure of the enormous sacrifices it had cost. He described how he questioned the generals during the last days of the war and asked them to explain to him the nature of the victory that had been won. They could not answer, he said. Even they, the generals who had won the victory, were forced to admit that they did not fully understand the moral forces that had moved their armies. They stood before a puzzle, the sphinx of victories. Only the critics, sneered Panferov, the "crocks and potsherds," as he called them, were able to understand this great imponderable.

For the "crocks and potsherds" all this is clear.

"Retreat? There was no retreat. This was a planned withdrawal that exhausted the enemy."

"But," asks the writer, "what kind of a planned withdrawal was this, when the fate of our country at one time hung by a hair? Indeed, Comrade Stalin and his fellow workers spoke to us about this."

"Forget it! It is necessary to forget this," answer the crocks and potsherds.

Forget how? Perhaps it is possible to forget that the Germans were at Stalingrad, at Mozdok, at Moscow? How is it possible to forget the burdens our people shouldered during the war? Indeed, sometimes our shoulders cracked under these burdens.[16]

Panferov then recalled the terrible hardships suffered by the working people in setting up the evacuated industries in the rear. He described the hard living conditions, the rigors of winter work in the Urals, the cold that froze the palms of the workers' hands to the steel. He contrasted this picture with the pretty formulas encouraged by official propaganda.

But here come the crocks and potsherds and insistently declare:

"Nonsense! Nothing like this happened in our country. This is the way it was—the workers arrived in the Urals and immediately were settled in the best cottages; pork chops were immediately placed on their tables; they went at once into warm shops, immediately found specifications, and began at once to 'fulfill and overfulfill.' "

The writer spreads his hands in perplexity. Indeed, he very well knows how, before the evacuation of certain industrial enterprises from Moscow, important members of the Central Committee of the Party appeared at the factories and plants and spoke to the workers about the number of difficulties they would have to bear, both on the way and at the new locations (in the Urals for example), about the fact that they would have to live in barracks, and construct shops from the ground up, in cold and storms. Our Party never concealed, nor does it now conceal, anything from our people; it always speaks only the truth, and teaches the writer to speak only the truth to the people. And yet the writer knows that things do not go as smoothly in life as even the writer himself would wish.[17]

Panferov cited a story, apparently recently published at that time, portraying the gay, contented hospital life of men who had been blinded at the front. "All this is written," he said, "so that it becomes rather thick for the reader—'Oh, why am I not also blind?' " When such blatant falsehoods as these are thrown up to the critics, said Panferov, they always retort that the readers demand such literature. Panferov defended the intelligence of the Soviet reader. The reader is not a nonparticipant "like you crocks and potsherds," he pointed out. "He was at the front, he retreated, attacked, and lived through terrors and joys. He worked at full strength at the rear, he lived through successes and failures." The reader is none other than the soldiers and workers who lived the truth in their daily lives. To deceive such a reader is a difficult matter.

It was in the midst of this discussion that Panferov launched his frontal attack on the critics. He described them as misfits, as parasites, as men who had stumbled into literature only because no other profession would have them. Needless to say, Erlikh was held up as an example of this type of man, who contributed nothing to society but prevented others from doing so.

What is the basic fault (and harm) of the crocks and potsherds? Why are they, these crocks and potsherds, not in the plants, the factories, on the kolkhozes? Why? Because in the factory they check up on work. You have made a good product—praise and honor to you. A bad product—this is waste. And they will give you such a drubbing that you will then look sharp and not turn out waste again. And if you cannot fit in at all, you leave the factory. There, in production work, the crocks and potsherds cannot survive. But among us they survive. . . .

Before us is an article by Erlikh. The reader certainly does not know him. But we know that Erlikh is already fifty years old, that for twenty years he has lived in the literary world . . . and that during these twenty years he has written essentially nothing but a little book of dull stories. Before us also is the last novel of Arkadiy Perventsev, *Flaming Land*. . . . This gifted writer conveys something to the reader that in some way enriches our still very young Soviet literature. He works like the majority of us, knowing that literature is created in a general stream, that we are all working out a new literary life, and that the time is coming when a genius writer will emerge from our preliminary work. We take pride in this. And in what may Erlikh take pride? For the fact that he has "existed" in literature for two or three decades? He will die—and over his grave they will place a membership card in the Union of Writers. And they will say about Erlikh:

"Here lies. . . . He contrived for two or three decades to live among the writers, and he wrote nothing."[18]

Returning to the issue of the war, Panferov concluded his article with a discussion of the character of the enemy and of the proper way of portraying the enemy in literature. He disputed the official tendency to deprecate the military qualities of the Germans. This, he argued, did no credit to the Soviet Army; in fact, it minimized the significance of the victory it had achieved. The crocks and potsherds, he said, insist that the enemy should be portrayed as stupid, cowardly, ignorant of military matters—in a word, as a "wooden head with eyes."

But, if you will, why minimize the strength of the enemy, his resourcefulness, his rapaciousness, his cunning, his military skill, his steadiness in battle, his ability to defend himself, to attack, and finally, to fight? Indeed, in depicting the enemy as a wooden head with eyes, we minimize the heroism of the Red Army. What kind of heroism is it to have beaten a wooden head with eyes? No, the enemy was strong, in his own way able, cunning, and steady in battle. Indeed, no wooden head with eyes could have seized, if only temporarily, the whole of Europe, and moved into our country hundreds of divisions armed from head to toe. No. And how explain the power of the enemy, his psychology—why millions went over to the fascists, if only for a time? To solve this is an extraordinarily complicated and necessary matter. . . .

Let the crocks and potsherds depict the enemy as a wooden head with eyes.[19]

It is easier to grasp the emotional impulse of Panferov's article than the rational objectives that motivated it. According to later criticism, which in this respect appears plausible, Panferov had for many years shown a strong tendency toward an empiric, emotional approach to life, and a contempt for theory. The critic scornfully quoted his words in this sense: " 'It is necessary in life to feel one's way with one's hands,' but not with the head, he says. 'Only oxen go up to a solid wall and butt it with their heads.' "[20] This contempt for "headwork," this predilection for immediate contact with life, was reflected in many passages of Panferov's article. It suggests a viewpoint more compatible with the early days of revolutionary experiment than the later days of "socialist construction," a bent of mind that would rankle under the strictures of rational or bureaucratic discipline. This temperamental intractability, combined with the pride that often attends a successful and influential career, undoubtedly contributed to the fire of Panferov's attack. But there was almost certainly more to Panferov's article than a mere rebellion against discipline.

The issue that provoked the article was the interpretation of the war, and there can be no doubt that Panferov passionately believed in the position he defended. Moreover, he seemed to feel that his viewpoint might prevail over the opposing view of the literary critics. He reminded his readers of the wartime words of Stalin and the Party leaders; he invoked the authority of the Party that "never concealed." In other words, when he published the article, Panferov seemed to regard the interpretation of the war as not yet a completely closed issue. The objective of his article, apparently, was to bully the critics and influence the political authorities behind them into accepting his interpretation of the role and responsibility of literature in portraying the history of the war. No doubt, active debates on this subject had been stimulated throughout the literary community by Stalin's electoral speech earlier in the year.

Apart from these calculations and circumstances, the lasting significance of Panferov's article rests in the testament it gave of Russia's wartime experience. On the eve of the postwar campaign of falsifications and half-truths, which the regime hoped would blot out the unhappy memories of the war, one clear voice bore witness to the sufferings and sacrifices it had cost. It spoke not only for Panferov, we may be sure, but for many of his colleagues as well, and indeed for the Russian people.

THE CASE OF TVARDOVSKIY'S NOTEBOOK

Echoes of this testimony to the truth about the war were to be heard again in the postwar period. In the last two issues of the literary journal *Banner,* in 1947, there appeared a work entitled "Motherland and Foreignland: Pages from a Notebook," by A. Tvardovskiy. In it, the poet attempted to re-create impressions from a lost wartime diary.[21] It presented a collection of vignettes of his wartime experiences, impressions of the individuals he had seen, and evocations of the moods he had felt. The personal record of a sensitive observer, not originally intended for publication, it presented a remarkably clear-eyed view of the human features of the Soviet people in the war.

Tvardovskiy was particularly attracted by the hardiness, the sheer survival ability, of individuals in war, and he returned to this theme repeatedly. This naturally caused him to deal with characters and motivations that official propaganda pretended not to see, and laid him open to the charge that he had generalized the untypical rather than the typical features of Soviet reality. Several of his characters will illustrate the focus of his interest and the reasons for this official displeasure.

Aunt Zoya, a woman from the Moscow suburbs, was the subject of one of his sketches. She had lived by her wits all her life and, by the same qualities, had managed to survive the hazards of war and maintain her household in relative comfort. Her greatest wartime achievement, and for this she was recognized as a true heroine by Tvardovskiy, was that she had saved her cow throughout all the bombings. There was little in her to inspire the admiration of a politically conscious writer—she had chosen to remain behind when the city was evacuated, her manner of life was dubious from the socialist standpoint, and her most elevated ambition was to maintain an ample supply of food and drink—but she was a genuine human being, and it was this quality, obviously, that caught Tvardovskiy's eye.[22]

Another character whom he described appreciatively was an old kulak who had become disillusioned with the Germans during the occupation and wished to return to the Soviet land. In a conversation with a worker from the army procurator's office who was making his way back to the front, the old man explained the reasons for his change of heart. "Did the Soviet power deprive me in those years of everything movable and immovable? Do not deny it—it deprived me. Was I in exile for two years? Two years to the day. And there are others who were—two, perhaps three, and even five years. All this is true. And all the same I say to you . . ."[23] And he pointed to the good educations that the Soviet regime had given his sons and the honorable places it had made for them in society. Moreover, he added, the Germans had not respected private property in any event. Tvardovskiy's character, it will be seen, was an interesting type, but hardly the kind to inspire a Soviet writer.

As in the above sketch, where the kulak spoke of his exile, Tvardovskiy's faithfulness to his characterizations led him to touch on subjects sensitive to Soviet official ears. He described one evening spent in a peasant cottage, where, after the host had said his evening prayers and gone to sleep, Tvardovskiy lay awake talking with his soldier companion, who said to him:

You know, all the places—where I was born, where I studied, where I served, where I settled down, and, in general, everywhere that I have been in life—are all under the Germans. Look, I was born in the Smolensk area and there lived until I was called into the army. Smolensk is no longer. I served for a time in Bobruisk, in Belorussia. Belorussia is no longer. I studied in Leningrad. Leningrad is encircled. Twice during my life I went to a rest home, both times in the Crimea, in the Yalta Home of Rest for Commanders. Yalta is no longer. Thus it is with everything. I have never had to go to the East. There remains for me only Moscow. True, I was there only on a train, but I was there nevertheless. And even Moscow is a front-line city.[24]

In addition to these sharp delineations of character, Tvardovskiy also conveyed a vivid impression of the broader social impact of the war. In a strikingly evocative passage, he described a scene of refugee disaster during the early days, a vast animal-like migration of people fleeing from the conflagration of war.

On the first page of the notebook, I remember, I wrote down a picture that struck me at the beginning of the war, in my first encounter with those on whom a heavy burden had fallen in the first days. The Moscow-Kiev train stopped at a station, apparently Khutor Mikhailovskiy. Looking out the window, I saw something so strange and frightening that, to this day, I cannot get rid of the impression. I saw a field, a huge field, but whether it was a meadow, a fallow field, a field sown to winter or spring crops, it was impossible to tell: The field was covered with people, lying, sitting, swarming, people with bundles, knapsacks, suitcases, hand carts, little children. I never saw so many suitcases, bundles, all kinds of village-household goods, hurriedly taken by people for a journey. On this field there were perhaps five, perhaps ten thousand people. . . . The field buzzed. And amidst this drone one could hear the agitation, the excitement caused by the recent shock, and, at the same time, the deep, sad weariness, the numbness, the half-sleep, that one observes in a crowded waiting room at night in a large railway junction. The field rose, began to stir, pushed toward the right of way, to the train, began to rap on the doors and windows of the cars, and, it seemed, had the power to knock the cars from the rails. The train moved. We, people in war, breaking the strict and necessary order, pulled into the car one woman, loaded down with bundles, holding in her hands her two children, aged three and five years. She was from Minsk, the wife of a commander, and coming into the car hastened to confirm this with documents. She was small, haggard, not at all beautiful, except perhaps her eyes, shining with the joy of unexpected success. She had to go somewhere in Belaya Tserkov, to the family of her husband. She could hardly have gotten there—a few days later I saw that Belaya Tserkov was abandoned by us.[25]

Tvardovskiy's honesty extended also to self-analysis and produced an unusually picturesque and unflattering account of the function of the writers in the war. Feeling the fatigue of his long tour of service, he asked himself why his mind faltered at the task of writing once again the story of seemingly endless battles. He compared himself and his fellow writers to a man who helped another to chop wood by grunting for each blow of the axe. "We grunt, and the people work. We have taken on ourselves the function . . . of giving out those exclamations, 'ohs' and 'ahs,' etc., that are those of the man who fights." For the soldier, each new battle summons up his mental and physical forces with the sharpness of original freshness. "But for us, grunting, all this is just more of the same thing; we have grunted for a thousand such occasions." However, he conceded that it was necessary to go on writing because of the magnificent victories that the soldiers were winning.[26]

The critical reaction to Tvardovskiy's notebook was swift and caustic. An article in Literary Gazette, in December, presented a biting review of the work. "The attempt to poeticize what is foreign to the life of the people and foreign to poetry has led to a false and crude ideological and artistic mistake."[27] A week later, an editorial in Literary Gazette reiterated the official anger: "The whole work is impregnated with a feeling of tiredness, pacifism, a contemplative attitude toward life. It is enough to say that Soviet writers and journalists, who gloriously fought on the fronts of the Great Patriotic War with pen and weapon, compare A. Tvardovskiy to a man who does nothing but 'grunt' while watching the people work."[28] Despite this strong official condemnation, the issue was not finally put to rest.

In February, 1948, Literary Gazette carried a brief report of a discussion on Tvardovskiy's notebook, containing hints that opposition to the official criticism had manifested itself among the writers. The report stated that the discussion had been put off three times and that on the fourth occasion, when it was finally held, the editorial board of Banner had absented itself from the meeting. In addition, the claim that the official evaluation of the work had been supported by the meeting was qualified: "The opinion of the majority of the speakers in large part coincided with . . ." [Italics added.] Finally, the open opposition of one speaker, a student from Moscow University, was acknowledged. Regarding this reaction, the report stated:

General agitation was called forth by the speech of a graduate student of Moscow University, V. Arkhipov. In an oily tone, he undertook to prove that there were no mistakes in "Motherland and Foreignland." Attempting by all means to protect A. Tvardovskiy from justified criticism, he ended up with openly reactionary declarations in defense of kulaks and speculators. The harmful expressions of the uninvited advocate were given a well-deserved reply in the speeches of S. L'vov, Z. Kedrin, and others.[29]

The case of Tvardovskiy's notebook illustrates the nature of the conflict between official and literary views regarding the portrayal of the war. The regime wished the war to be presented as an idealized epic; the writers wished to present it as a real, believable human achievement. The response of the writers to Tvardovskiy's honesty in the present case—which was almost certainly more spontaneous and sympathetic than the official press admitted—demonstrated the resistance the official line continued to meet long after the general issue of the interpretation of the war had been settled. That this resistance may have been inspired more by artistic than conscious political objectives in no way diminishes the political courage of men such as Arkhipov, who were willing to stand openly for their convictions against the official power of the literary bureaucracy.

"The Motorship 'Kakhetia' " and the Intervention of Vershigora

While Tvardovskiy's work was being discussed, another war-time memoir was being published that was to set off an even more dramatic demonstration of opposition to the official line on the war. This was the diary of Olga Dzhigurda, a military doctor, which appeared in the first two issues of *Banner* in 1948, under the title "The Motorship 'Kakhetia.' "[30] In the ensuing discussion of this diary, in which marked discontent with the official critical evaluation was recorded, Petro Vershigora, the famous partisan leader, Stalin Prize winner, and author of *Men With a Clear Conscience*, published a strong attack on the critics for encouraging a hypocritical portrayal of the war instead of the honest accounts the people's sacrifices deserved. In the vigor and directness of its attack, Vershigora's article came close to matching the ardor of Panferov's polemic of two years before.

The diary of Dzhigurda, which precipitated the dispute, was itself a patently honest portrayal of the thoughts, feelings, and behavior of people exposed to war. It recorded the author's experiences as a military doctor on a supply-hospital ship in 1941–42, serving the besieged city of Sevastopol and other military bases. In simple, straightforward language, the author describes the people around her, neither embellishing their virtues nor concealing their faults. At the very beginning, she unashamedly admits the reluctance with which she and her companions approached their assignment to the ship. "In vain, Belokon and Vetrova entreated the duty officer to send us to some land unit; in vain, Vetrova tried to frighten the duty officer with big names from the air forces; in vain, I complained of my seasickness."[31]

Dzhigurda saw and graphically recorded the variety of human emotions displayed by her companions when subjected to the test of war. For example, there was the chief surgeon, who always lost control of herself as soon as the air alert was sounded. "From a smart commander, she was instantly transformed into a pitiable woman, trembling with fear: she shook, she wrung her hands, cried, and wailed." There was the apothecary, who found refuge in drink. "Before a battle, he always headed for the 'aqua vitae,' or as we called it, 'the antibomb fluid'. . . . Having drunk, Ukhov became unusually tender, his eyes moistened, and he began to talk expansively about some elevated subject." There was the surgeon's assistant, who had already lived through two sinkings and who found some kind of strange relief in talking about death. "Usually taciturn, he began to babble without stopping during raids and air battles. His stories were terrifying—battle episodes that invariably ended with someone's death or some such catastrophe."[32]

Dzhigurda's reportorial accuracy led her to record events that were highly "untypical" by Soviet official standards. The captain of the ship, for example, suffered a nervous breakdown and committed suicide. Two soldiers evacuated from Sevastopol turned out to be malingerers. "What will become of them?" Dzhigurda asked, as they were being led away. "They will be shot [or] sent to a penal battalion," she was told.[33] Once her roommate's sobbing woke her in the night.

"What's the matter? What's the matter with you?" I asked anxiously.

"I cannot be alone! It's boring to be alone!" Vetrova wailed through her tears.

I was upset.

"Listen, Marya Afanas'yevna, aren't you ashamed? Just a few days before the trip, and all you think about is foolishness. We have to fight with pure thoughts and a pure spirit, and all you think about is men!"

"I'm pregnant," suddenly groaned Vetrova, and fell on the pillow and cried.[34]

These "untypical" features of the diary, needless to say, scandalized official opinion. Dzhigurda was accused of having failed to bring out the real spirit of the Soviet people, of having lost herself in details. "It is not necessary to minimize the personal shortcomings of our people," said E. Knipovich, writing in *Literary Gazette*. "But if one is to see the main, socialist thing above all, then the petty, personal shortcomings are not blown up disproportionately."[35] In the April issue of *Star,* the critic Lifshits pronounced

an even sterner verdict on the diary.[36] These official views, however, were not shared by the readers.

A discussion of the diary was held early in May, 1948. The
animation of the proceedings, the enthusiastic support for Dzhigurda that they demonstrated, came through even in the cryptic
report of the affair published in *Literary Gazette*.[37] A remarkable
feature of the meeting was that it appeared to be organized by,
and certainly provided a forum for, "people of experience," that is,
those who like Dzhigurda herself had actually participated in the
war. This, then, unlike the discussion of Tvardovskiy's notebook,
was not simply a literary meeting, but a broader public demonstration.

The session was opened by Petro Vershigora, who described
the broad, enthusiastic response the diary had evoked.

The editorial board of *Banner*, the Union of Writers, the newspapers,
are receiving many letters. . . . Sailors, doctors, people of the most
different professions are organizing discussions, arguing about the
achievements and shortcomings of the diary. Already, this testifies to
the fact that "The Motorship 'Kakhetia' " is not an ordinary event in
our literature.

The central theme of praise reiterated by the speakers at the
meeting was the honesty of Dzhigurda's work. One spoke about
the "true, acute, unadorned observations" of the author; another
hailed the absence of "a beauty parlor touching-up" of reality;
another praised the "rare capacity of the author to write from
nature, from the living man." The few critical observations made
were reportedly disputed on the spot.

The number of military figures present, and speaking on Dzhigurda's behalf, was perhaps the most notable feature of the meeting. Major General P. Musyakov, editor of the newspaper *Red
Fleet,* said that he could testify from personal experience to the
truth of Dzhigurda's work. He said that he knew personally many

people from the "Kakhetia" and had met others indirectly through his newspaper work during the siege of Sevastopol. "There are documents, unknown to the author, that speak about the same days and events. They confirm the vitality of the diary." Another prominent military figure, Colonel D. Kornienko, Deputy Chief of the Political Administration of the Navy, offered to help the author by showing her documents that could enrich her material. The support of these officers, influential representatives of military opinion, to say nothing of the initiative of Vershigora himself, undoubtedly goes far to explain how a demonstration of such open opposition to the literary bureaucracy could have been possible.

In the following month, Vershigora published his formal attack on the critics. He described their reception of Dzhigurda's work as flowing from the consistently negative attitude they had shown toward eyewitness accounts of the war. The object of his attack was to refute not simply the official evaluation of one work, but the whole system of official attitudes that had determined this evaluation. His indictment exposed the nature of the campaign the critics had waged to substitute platitudinous formulas for honest accounts of the war.

Pseudo-classical conceptions regarding Soviet people at war and the motives for their actions and encounters have apparently nurtured sanctimonious ideals in the critics themselves. And the critics (according to the laws of a certain reverse diffusion, perhaps) react sharply to any departure from these lacquered norms. Pharisaical critics give battle surreptitiously, without undue noise, to the genre of "experience": they avoid raising the question to the level of principle, so to speak, ignore the early diaries of front-line people, or note superficially their weaknesses, and, above all, disparage their significance.[38]

Vershigora then produced evidence to show that the ordinary people, the readers, shared his views. He quoted letters received by the editorial board of *Banner* praising the work of Dzhigurda.

He accused the critics of persecuting Dzhigurda precisely because she had given an honest account of the "complex, and sometimes contradictory, phenomena of wartime reality."

Not wishing to prettify the events of the first, difficult, and often tragic period of the war, the author evidently calls forth protest and disparagement only from those who avoid the living truth and prefer an oleograph to a fearlessly true story about the complex, and sometimes contradictory, phenomena of wartime reality. The author did not wish to give a lofty, didactic character to her diary. She simply tells how things were in one small part of the war and the impressions that these days and events, so memorable to all of us, left on her soul. And at the end, she receives her "reward": from Comrade Lifshits, who scrupulously recorded the moral "sins" of Comrade Dzhigurda, literally as in a police report, and from Comrade Knipovich, who had recourse, in the pages of *Litgazet,* to long citations from the work of the experienced writer Comrade Simonov and to my work, presumably to pummel more heavily, with citations and names, an author who had the temerity to mention such "untypical" phenomena as a general's "army camp wife."[39]

Vershigora cited the paucity of literature on the siege of Leningrad as an example of the deadly influence exercised by the critics. He said that after 1944, an honest portrayal of this great event had become impossible. He spoke of one "highly placed conference" devoted to literature on the war, at which one writer justifiably complained that he had not been able to write the truth about the feat of Leningrad "since the literary and critical channels filled up with people who never had a taste of blockade."

Every attempt to describe the blockade is taken by them as slander against the Leningrad people. The almost complete absence of great literature on the worthy and necessary theme of the heroic defense of Leningrad convinces me that the aforementioned comrade is right. Crude facts (and they are always crude, particularly for those who have not had a whiff of them) cannot be written, and people are apparently still ashamed to write the prettified "little truths," which are always worse than open lies. And the result? The needed book about the great feat of Leningrad has not, and does not, come![40]

Finally, Vershigora asserted the bold claim that "defenders of the Fatherland" had the moral right to share their experiences of the war with their contemporaries. He predicted, moreover, that such firsthand accounts would not be forgotten when the history of the war was finally written.

Our contemporaries, who, shoulder to shoulder, have forged the victory, as well as future generations studying the past, will look into them. They will have to look into them! Surely, the many novels, stories, poems, and books, which are less finished in literary style but more convincing, not only by virtue of the facts they contain, but also by their *faithfulness to the human feelings* they portray, will not be thrown into the backyard of history.[41]

The dispute over Dzhigurda's diary is the most significant case we have examined, because of the light it throws on the nature of the internal tensions created by the official version of the history of the war. It shows that opposition to the official platitudes on the history of the war was felt by fairly broad and disparate elements of the Soviet population. It confirms the inference that logic suggested, but which the military press supported only inconclusively—that a significant segment of military opinion shared this negative reaction. Finally, it provides a valuable insight into the character of the official propaganda campaign itself. Vershigora's charge that the critics acted "surreptitiously, without undue noise," and avoided raising the issue to the level of "principle," could as appropriately have been applied to the behavior of the propaganda machine as a whole as to the literary bureaucracy alone. The official history of the war, as everything we have seen tends to confirm, was propagated more by indirection and innuendo than by the more usual methods of bandwagon publicity.

The fact that prominent opponents of the official line suffered no immediate or open reprisal for their temerity testifies to the noiselessness of the campaign and the disinclination of the authorities to draw attention to embarrassing issues. Panferov and Tvardovskiy continued to occupy responsible posts in the literary hierarchy; Vershigora suffered only gradual neglect. Despite this forbearing treatment, however, all of these men continued to show signs of stubborn independence in the following years. Tvardovskiy was the editor of *New World* when it published the revisionary article of Pomerantsev, "On Sincerity in Literature," in 1953, and, condemned for the arrogance he showed in ignoring the criticism of this article and for the policies of his magazine in general, he was dismissed as editor.[42] Panferov, despite more than the ordinary share of critical vicissitudes, remained at the helm of *October* until 1954, when his path crossed Vershigora's again, with unfortunate results for him. He gave space in his journal to an article by Vershigora, entitled "Brothers in Arms," which carried a footnote criticizing the Ukrainian Academy of Science's official history of the Ukraine for its slighting treatment of the Cossacks and charging the editors of that text with a lack of Ukrainian patriotism.[43] The upshot was that Panferov was fired from his job as editor of *October* and came very close to being linked with Virta, Surov, and others, who were dismissed from the Writers Union at that time for moral turpitude.[44] Vershigora's decline was apparently more subtle. It can be traced, for example, in successive editions of the official history textbook for the tenth class of the secondary schools. In the 1948 edition, he was named as one of the *three* "outstanding partisan leaders." In the 1951 edition, he was named as one of *four* "notable commanders and organizers." In the 1957 edition, his name no longer appeared in the relevant passage.[45]

These facts suggest a more general observation, which may serve as a concluding commentary on this chapter. The writing community, as a whole, demonstrated a chronic indiscipline after the war, which was unmatched by any other segment of Soviet society. The sources of this indiscipline were perhaps as various as the individuals who, for their own reasons—vanity, stubbornness, artistic integrity, etc.—sustained and nurtured it. But two other factors—one pertaining to the nature of literature itself, the other to the conditions of literary work in the Soviet Union—contributed to this intransigeance. Writers, by the very nature of their work, deal with human motivation and human relationships in terms comprehensible to themselves and acceptable to their readers. The subject of the writer's work is man—man, and not Soviet man—and Soviet writers, like all writers everywhere, are concerned with the universal human values that motivate man's behavior and the weaknesses that condition his existence. The writer, in his own mind at least, has to grapple with the great problems of human life—with love and death—and the shallow political philosophy that the Soviet writer was asked to serve failed to explain, or even acknowledge, these problems. The Soviet writer was thrust into a world of perceptions as broad as human history itself, and, insofar as he absorbed and reflected these perceptions in his work, he became a witness to the universality of human nature and human experience, which official philosophy denied. Thus, tension between his political loyalty and his loyalty to his art became a permanent attribute of the writer's work in the Soviet Union.

Secondly, the conditions of literary work in the Soviet Union gave Soviet writers the facilities to press continually for a resolution of this tension. The partial editorial independence enjoyed by literary journals encouraged writers to probe for the outer limits of official tolerance and permitted them to express views that a stricter censorship would have prevented. This helped to keep alive the sense of a shared problem and contributed to a feeling of group identity among the writers. The self-identity of the writers' community undoubtedly encouraged a degree of individual inde-

pendence that real independence, i.e., isolation, would have de-
pressed.

The opposition the writers showed to the official history of
the war was, in this light, an aspect of a more general phenomenon.
It testified to the writers' inability as artists to portray the great
human experience of the war within the untruthful formulas
required by official propaganda.

6

The Post-Stalin Reappraisal of the History of the War

The flurry of opposition to the official history of the war that we have observed was snuffed out by 1949, and, for several years thereafter, a deep freeze of Stalinist orthodoxy settled over this issue. Occasional criticisms of individual authors during this period were indicative more of the insatiability of critical appetites than of any real indiscipline on the part of the authors thus singled out. One index of the solidification of the official line was the increasing attention devoted to the history of the war by the press and publishing houses, which registered the propagandists' conviction that the subject had become stable and safe. But history in the Soviet Union was no more stable than the political forces that projected it, and with Stalin's death, the image of his power, reflected in history, began to fade. The ensuing reappraisal of the history of the war—its processes and results—is the subject of this chapter.

THE IMPACT OF STALIN'S DEATH

The natural disintegrative process of the Stalinist historical myths that began with the death of the old dictator was accelerated by the problems the new government faced. These were of two kinds. First, there was the succession itself: The new system of collective leadership had to be legitimized and shored up with historical sanctions; the state administration, pulverized by Stalin, had to be reconstituted; long-suppressed consumer demands had to be satisfied; a way out of the foreign-policy impasse to which Stalin's blustering policies had led the Soviet Union had to be found. Secondly, there were problems arising from the military-strategic situation created by the maturing of nuclear developments within the Soviet Union and by the continuing improvement of delivery capabilities in both world-power blocs. The solutions that suggested themselves for these problems had a common implication: a break with Stalinist tradition, and, indirectly, with the historical myths in which these traditions had become embedded.

The effects of the new policy on the first group of problems were apparent almost immediately. The "cult of personality" was disparaged and the "creativity of the masses" extolled. To be sure, the effect was less marked and less consistent in historical writing on the war, but there were unmistakable shifts in emphasis. Stalin's name appeared less frequently where one had become accustomed to find it, and the Party, falling heir to his hagiographical attributes, was put forward as the supreme architect of victory. The role of the people in the war was also accorded a recognition that befitted their newly acknowledged status as the "creators of history." The Central Committee document published in July, 1953, on the fiftieth anniversary of the Party, which portrayed the war as a triumph of Party policy and ignored Stalin, provided a capsule illustration of this new emphasis.[1]

More important and longer-lasting implications for the history of the war emerged from the second set of problems mentioned above—the reassessment of Soviet military-strategic policies that accompanied the new leadership's break with Stalin. As men who had been close to the summit of Soviet power for many years, the

new leaders were certainly not unacquainted with the strategic
problems posed by the increasing destructiveness of world arma-
ments. But the responsibilities of supreme authority, the removal
of Stalin's inhibiting influence, the new evidence that piled up
during 1953 as a result of the Soviet Union's first hydrogen-bomb
explosion, and the beginning in military maneuvers of that year to
readjust the Soviet Army to nuclear warfare undoubtedly cast these
problems in a new light.[2] In any event, clear signs of a more
realistic attitude toward the military implications of the nuclear
age were manifested. The seven-year ban on the discussion of
nuclear weapons was broken in 1954, when *Red Star* began a
series of articles on the tactical uses of the new weapons and defenses against them. During the same period, a broad discussion
of military science, reflecting strong tendencies toward a rejuvena-
tion of military thought, was carried on in the General Staff journal,
Military Thought.

On the political level, the impact of the new strategic situation
was reflected in Malenkov's efforts to damp down the sparks that
might set off an international conflagration. That concern with the
danger of a possible nuclear war was a basic influence in his policy
was attested to by Malenkov himself in his famous declaration of
1954 that a new world war would mean the "destruction of world
civilization."[3] The circumstances surrounding this declaration
strongly suggest that Malenkov meant it as a powerful argument
in defense of his policies. It was made just one week after the first
open opposition to his regime had been signalized in the Soviet
press.[4] It was a carefully calculated statement, since it revised a
long-held, often-repeated Soviet doctrine, which Malenkov himself
had helped formulate,[5] that a new war would mean the destruction
of world capitalism. The indications are strong that it expressed not
only his own belief in the unacceptability of nuclear war but his
hope that others within the Soviet Union, the lesser Party leaders
and intellectuals to whom his words were undoubtedly addressed,

would be persuaded by the same reasoning to accept his view.*

Malenkov's specific prescription for Soviet policy in the nuclear age was repudiated when he resigned in February, 1955, but the military-strategic considerations that had given rise to it continued to preoccupy his successors. Moreover, by placing the military in a temporarily more independent position, the power struggle by which the Bulganin-Khrushchev succession was engineered had the effect of stimulating the tendencies toward a fresh look at military realities that the Malenkov regime had initiated. The return of experienced military officers to high administrative posts in the defense establishment, which had been going on since the last year of Stalin's life, and particularly the appointment of Marshal Zhukov as Minister of Defense, in February, 1955, further accelerated these tendencies. During the next few months, the greater degree of professionalism and realism that these developments had brought to the sphere of military thought resulted in important revisions in military doctrine and military history.

The harbinger of the new era in military thought was an article by Marshal of Tank Troops Rotmistrov, which appeared in the February issue of *Military Thought,* revising the reigning Soviet doctrine on the significance of the surprise factor in war.[6] Ever since the early days of the war, when Stalin propounded his doc-

---

* A curious ideological controversy, which flared up shortly before Malenkov's statement, suggested that the concerns that had moved him to his unorthodox prognosis of the results of a nuclear war had also stirred intellectual circles. An article in *Zvezda,* in November, 1953, by M. Gus, argued that the Marxist doctrine of the inevitability of war was simply an expression of regularities rather than a statement of fatal inevitability. By knowing the law, man was placed in the position of being able to curtail it, to limit its application. Thus, Gus implied, the law of the inevitability of war did not necessarily mean that the Soviet Union would become involved in a nuclear war with the West. Although this view was swiftly repudiated (*Kommunist,* No. 1, 1954, and *Zvezda,* No. 2, 1954), the subject was broached again, by Leontyev, in September (*Kommunist,* No. 13, 1954), and Varga, in October (*New Times,* No. 41, 1954). Both made efforts to reach the same comforting conclusions as Gus, but in ideologically less objectionable ways.

trine of the permanently operating factors that determine the outcome of war, the significance of the surprise factor had been deprecated in Soviet military theory. In the wartime propaganda and subsequently, the early successes of the Germans were ascribed to the "temporary" factor of surprise, which had no significance for the final outcome of the war once the permanently operating factors (the stability of the rear, the morale of the army, the quantity and quality of divisions, the armament of the army, the organizational abilities of the commanding staff) came into play. In Rotmistrov's article, for the first time, the relationship between the permanently operating factors and the temporary factors (of which surprise was the principal one) was clearly shifted to heighten the significance of the latter. For the first time, the factor of surprise was accorded a significance that the era of nuclear weapons and transcontinental bombers made prudent and necessary. The reasons for this shift of doctrine were explained some years later by a military author writing in *Red Star*. "The appearance of nuclear weapons," he said, "and the possibility for their mass employment against troops and targets in the rear, produced different opinions on the significance of the surprise attack in a future war and on measures for opposing such an attack. This prompted some military writers to engage in an investigation of the significance of the factor of surprise in modern war."[7] Marshal Rotmistrov, it seems, was the first to have the courage to voice the opinions these considerations produced in him. Subsequent developments showed that he was not alone in his views.

The military-strategic considerations discussed above, and the doctrinal revision they produced, provide a basis for understanding the next stage in the development of Soviet official views on the war. The interconnection of the doctrine of the permanently operating factors and the official interpretation of the first period of the war made it inevitable that the revision of the former would affect the latter. In addition, there were strong practical reasons, arising from the same considerations that had prompted the revision of doctrine, for changing the picture of the first period of the war heretofore presented to Soviet readers.

THE REVISIONARY MOVEMENT OF 1955

The revision of the history of the war that took place in 1955 was a direct result of the military-strategic revaluations under examination here. It reflected the apprehension of the Soviet leaders that the unrealistic, propagandistic portrayal of the last war had not prepared the Soviet people and the military establishment for the type of warfare that had now become a possibility. This propaganda, they felt, encouraged the dangerous illusion that war was easy and conditioned military officers to feel that retreats and slow attritional methods were normal means of conducting war. In other words, the official history of the war compounded the errors committed by Soviet military doctrine. As *Military Thought* put it at that time, and as was to be reiterated in other writings during the year, the official history had led "not only to the distortion of the actual military events of 1941, but to the idealization of this form of combat, and incorrectly orients our military cadres to the possibilities of repeating it in a future war."[8]

The first full statement of the new version of the war that these considerations produced appeared in a lead editorial of *Military Thought,* in March, 1955.[9] This article breathed a spirit of root-and-branch revision of the old Stalinist dogmas. The main thesis presented was that fresh and original thought was needed to keep the Soviet military establishment responsive to the demands of contemporary military realities. It condemned the slavish attitude toward Stalin that, it said, obtained among military writers, as the main obstacle to creative developments in this sphere. It asked scornfully why Stalin's thesis on the permanently operating factors should have been considered a new contribution to military science. "Why was this permitted?" it asked. "For no other reason than that our military-scientific workers, academicians, military editors, and our military press are afraid to call things by their right names and say anything new."[10] The editors of *Military Thought* themselves, the editorial admitted, shared this guilt. They had held back the publication of Rotmistrov's article on surprise in warfare because of their fear of posing new questions.

The main content of the new version of the war that this article defined, and later articles elaborated, was that the early period of the war was a defeat for the Soviet Army rather than a prelude to victory. Criticism focused on the doctrine of "active defense," on the old official claim that the operations of the first period of the war had been preplanned and skillfully applied to bring about the defeat of the enemy. In fact, there never was such a plan, it was now admitted. "What the case was in fact we all well remember. Our experiences in that period, so desperate for our country, are sufficiently fresh in our memories." The doctrine of active defense, it was stated, concealed the mistakes that had been committed during that period and the defeats that had been suffered. It also denied due credit to the soldiers and people for their patriotism, courage, and staunchness, and to the commanding personnel for their skill. "It is necessary to put an end to this mistaken concept of the initial period of the war as quickly as possible, since in fact most of the operations of that period had the character of withdrawal operations."[11]

The impetus to revision that this article set in motion carried somewhat beyond the program it defined. Two months later, the second period of the war was being subjected to critical review as well. Colonel General P. Kurochkin, writing in the May issue of *Military Thought,* found glossing and oversimplification in the way the "ten Stalinist crushing blows" had been presented in official historical literature. Only a few of these operations, he said, were carried out according to plan. Some took longer than expected, others developed into operations larger than had been foreseen.[12] Kurochkin also presented the Stalingrad battle in an unusual way, in that he gave no indication that German strategy had aimed at the envelopment of Moscow.[13]

Stalin's role in the war was naturally affected by this revisionary movement, although the deprecation of his services did not proceed as far as certain statements in the original *Military Thought* editorial had seemed to imply. He continued to be accorded honor as the head of the country and the leader of the armed forces, although the adulatory phrases of past propaganda were toned down or removed. Kurochkin provided a precise formula on how the new history allocated the credits for victory among the major political elements of Soviet society.

The Communist Party of the Soviet Union was the leading and directing force in the heroic struggle of the Soviet people against the German fascist aggressors and raised outstanding commanders, who, headed by J. V. Stalin, demonstrated strategic and operational leadership. . . . The fundamental creator of the victory over fascist Germany . . . was the Soviet people.[14]

Finally, the role of the Allies in the war was broached indirectly in the new history. This, however, did not reflect concern for fairness or honesty, but rather the practical desirability of knowing the strengths and weaknesses of a possible future enemy. The original *Military Thought* editorial condemned the ideological inhibitions that had conditioned Soviet military writers to look upon non-Marxist literature as beneath their attention. "It is necessary decisively to condemn such a view. This is nothing but pride and arrogance."[15] Clearly, the editorial's concern in this matter was dictated by the same practical considerations that had prompted its attack on the official interpretation of the war. "It should be sufficiently clear to everyone that it is impossible to develop national military science without knowing well the military-theoretical views of the adversary."[16] In general, the revisionary movement of 1955 involved no softening of the traditional stance toward the

West; indeed, compared with the preceding two years, some hardening of attitudes accompanied it.

While these developments were taking place in the closed circle of military specialists, a somewhat blurred version of the revised history was being presented to the Soviet people. The presentation was complicated by confusions and conflicts generated by the recent political upheaval. The stimulus to factionalism within the upper reaches of the Soviet hierarchy that had accompanied the change of government, and the temporary slackening of political control that had followed it, posed an invitation to politically inclined military leaders to maneuver for position in the new regime. The historical interpretation of the war provided one platform on which this maneuvering could be done, since allegiance to one or another political leader could be indicated via the manner in which the war was treated. The fact that the Khrushchev faction, in its struggle with Malenkov, for tactical reasons had associated its program with Stalinist symbols left an opening for those who wished to declare their loyalty to Khrushchev; they could do so by resisting any revision of the history of the war that had anti-Stalinist implications. This was presumably the reason why some military leaders, particularly Marshal Konev, in his speech at the Bolshoi Theater on the Tenth Anniversary of victory, made little or no concession to the new interpretation of the war. On the whole, however, the majority of articles appearing at this time showed some influence of the revisionary movement.

A clearer indication of the import of the new movement was given to the two groups of particular concern in this study—the writers and the historians. At the end of May, 1955, a meeting of writers was held to explain the role of the "man with a gun" at the contemporary stage of world history, and the responsibilities of literature in presenting that role, and in cultivating the soldierly and civic virtues supporting it. An essential element of this explanation was the presentation of the revised view of the war that these practical considerations had produced among the military theorists themselves. The meeting was sponsored by the Union of Writers, but it was obviously initiated by the Main Political Administration of the Ministry of Defense. The keynote was sounded by the deputy chief of the Main Political Administration, Lieutenant General Shatilov, in an article that appeared in *Literary Gazette* on the eve of the meeting.[17]

Shatilov placed great emphasis throughout on the danger of attack by the West and on the greatly increased peril to the Soviet Union posed by the existence of the new nuclear weapons and improved delivery systems. This, he said, gave new significance to the question of surprise in war and required a more careful consideration of the role of surprise in the past. In particular, he said, it was necessary to show how the surprise factor had dominated the first period of the last war, since a false portrayal of this period might encourage erroneous notions about the nature of a future war.

In connection with this, it is necessary to point out that in our literature devoted to the Great Patriotic War, the first period of military operations is often idealized, portrayed as a period of operations conceived in classic forms as a so-called "active defense," and authors, contradicting real facts, attempt to depict the matter as though this "active defense" had been planned ahead of time and had entered into the calculations of our command. . . . A primitive interpretation of the initial period of the war, which distorts living reality wherever it takes place—in scientific works or in artistic works—cannot be tolerated, since it distorts historical truth and incorrectly orients our people, creating the impression that such precedents might, and even should, be repeated in the future.[18]

The published reports of the main speakers and the reports of the sessions presented reiterations of this theme, and also a hint or two of reactions stimulated in the writing community by the new atmosphere. A reaction against the personality cult appeared, for example, in criticism of Bubennov's *White Birch,* one of the most

notable examples of the adulatory style of Stalinist war literature.
A fairly open criticism of the literary bureaucracy was voiced by
V. Rudniy, a man who two years later was to emerge as one of
the leaders of the liberalizing movement among the Moscow writers.
He complained of the barriers that were raised against any attempt
to give a realistic portrayal of a military commander. "Because
as soon as we permit a divisional commander to begin to defend
his point of view, it means that he is refuting, to some degree, the
point of view of his superior, and a strict editor considers this a
breach in the stability of authority."[19] But mainly, the sessions bore
an official stamp (an impression enhanced by the absence of the
principal wartime writers, e.g., Simonov, Grossman, Leonov), and
the meeting was chiefly significant as a sounding board for the new
official line.

The historians received their briefing on the new interpretation
of the war in the lead editorial of *Questions of History* in May.[20]
This was the first formal public directive for a thorough review
of the history of the war, and in some respects it went beyond the
program of revision outlined in the military press. Besides repeating
the by now standard call for a revision of the accounts of the first
period of the war, it also demanded a downgrading of the Moscow
and Stalingrad battles (because describing them as turning points
of the war tended to diminish the significance of the Kursk and
subsequent battles) and urged a fuller account of the role of the
Allies. The latter point was qualified, however, by the linked argument that this would help dispel the "reactionary falsifications of
history" promoted by the imperialist press. Finally, it spelled out
the reasons for this call for revision:

Study and popularization of the history of the Great Patriotic War
will help strengthen the Soviet people's military preparedness to crush
any imperialist aggressor, and will help further to train the Soviet people in unshakable faith in the victory of their just cause and in ardent
Soviet patriotism and proletarian internationalism.[21]

This article was the principal manifesto of the revisionary movement in 1955. During the rest of the year there were few signs that the revision was being pursued vigorously, although another article by Rotmistrov, in November, showed that the theoretical considerations affecting the surprise factor, which had provoked the historical revision in the first place, continued to prevail in military circles.[22] The *Essays on the History of the Great Patriotic War*,[23] drafted before these events but permitted to come out later in the year, showed little effects of the 1955 revisionary movement. This, together with the general disappearance of the issue from the Soviet press, suggests that cautionary political influences, as well as irresolution within the collective leadership on Stalin's role in history, had resulted in slowing down the revision of the history of the war. But this was only a temporary pause, as events of the following year were to show. As the Twentieth Party Congress approached, new tendencies toward a break with the past appeared. These new currents gave fresh impetus to a reconsideration of the history of the war.

THE REVISIONARY MOVEMENT OF 1956

The revisionary movement of 1956 was both a continuation of past events and a new phenomenon. It followed along the channels cut by the military historians of 1955; but it was sponsored and sustained by new forces, and it served goals broader than the military-strategic considerations that had defined the earlier initiative. Moreover, it generated a momentum that carried it beyond the limits envisioned by the official revision of 1955, and, indeed, beyond the designs of the official sponsors of 1956. It was less calculated, less official, more spontaneous, than the revisionary movement of 1955.

The central thrust of the new movement was the general break with Stalin, dramatized by the Twentieth Party Congress. Although a gradual withdrawal from Stalinist traditions and Stalinist methods of leadership had been taking place since 1953, and although cautious downgradings of Stalin's historical role had accompanied this process, no clear and definitive disavowal of Stalin had been attempted. These factors had created tensions within the Soviet Union. In the first place, an incompatibility had grown between the rejuvenating policies the regime wished to pursue and the administrative habits engrained in the Soviet system by Stalin's autocracy and perpetuated by the continued aura of respectability surrounding his historical role. Secondly, the leaders had become increasingly aware of the double image of Stalin that was being retained —one for themselves and another for the lower cadres—and their discomfort with this inconsistency had been sharpened by the investigation of Stalin's crimes, secretly begun in 1955. Finally, the Stalinist tradition hung like a Damoclean sword over the new leadership, threatening, as long as factionalism existed in the government and Stalinist precedents could be invoked, to frustrate the consolidation of stable authority. Khrushchev's secret speech resolved these tensions by destroying Stalin's reputation. Whether his move was long planned or forced upon him by developments at the Twentieth Party Congress is irrelevant here. It was clear that the denigration of Stalin had been placed on the agenda by the logic of events.

Strong tendencies toward the revaluation of the Stalinist historical legacy appeared even before the Twentieth Party Congress opened, assuming a programmatic character at the conference of the readers of *Questions of History,* which was held at the end of January, 1956.[24] Accurately anticipating the mood of the Congress, which was to convene two weeks later, the conference outlined a revisionary program touching upon a broad range of established Soviet historical attitudes. Stalin's name appears not to have been mentioned in the leading speeches; Lenin was repeatedly extolled as the source of Soviet historical traditions; implicit criticism of Stalin's textbook on the history of the Party (the *Short Course*) was advanced; the cult of personality in history was condemned.

Even sacrosanct Soviet historical attitudes—toward the bourgeoisie in Europe and in Russia and toward the intra-Party struggles of the pre-Revolutionary and Revolutionary periods—were affected by the revisionary impulse. The reports of the conference made clear that a core of liberalizing historians, led by E. N. Burdzhalov, the deputy editor of *Questions of History*, was preparing to dismantle a large part of the historical scaffolding that had been erected around Stalin's image.

The history of the war was one part of the historical legacy brought up for review, although it was not a major preoccupation of the conference. Burdzhalov touched on the subject briefly in his broad-ranging critique of past historical attitudes and complained that "the difficulties of the first period" had not been revealed in standing works on the war.[25] More relevant to the main thrust of his argument, and also carrying implications for the history of the war, was his call for a fresh approach to the study of the West. "The U.S.A. has progressive as well as reactionary traditions," he noted. Others indicated their favorable attitude toward a new history of the war by praising the revisionary editorial that had appeared in *Questions of History* in 1955.[26] Still others complained of the situation that had prevailed in the past: the closing of the military historical section of the History Institute,[27] the inaccessibility of archive documents,[28] the "schematization, vulgarization, departure from historical truth, the idealization of past military figures, the personality cult,"[29] that had characterized military history.

The Twentieth Party Congress gave a vigorous impetus to this movement not only by giving it official auspices, but also by supplying the substantive criticism of Stalin that had served as the solvent of traditional historical attitudes. Khrushchev's secret speech, which portrayed Stalin as ignorant of military matters and as criminally responsible for the initial unpreparedness of the Soviet Union as well as for subsequent defeats, was quickly made known to Party members and, indirectly, to the politically literate elements of the Soviet population. Beginning a few weeks after the adjournment of the Congress and continuing for several months thereafter, the Soviet press gave numerous signs of the shock impact these revelations had had throughout the Soviet Union. Reports of lower Party meetings, which began to appear on March 19, and a rash of editorials on the themes of "Party unity" and "Leninist principles" were liberally sprinkled with angry charges against "rotten elements," "demagogues," "Leftists," etc., who were allegedly using the revelations as pretexts for attacks against the Party.

One charge in particular stood out and was particularly relevant to future developments in the historiography of the war. This was the charge that Party members had used the denigration of Stalin as a vehicle for the disparagement of all authority in general and the Soviet form of one-man command in particular. From early April until as late as August, the Party press repeatedly fulminated against those who denied "all authorities in general,"[30] who sought to undermine "Party discipline,"[31] who expressed a "petty-bourgeois denial of the role of leaders in state, Party, and economic work,"[32] who denied the "principle of one-man leadership,"[33] who attempted "to minimize the role of authority,"[34] etc. The critic Gribachev, writing in *Izvestia*, alluded to the nature of the social turbulence that had evoked these expressions of concern.

And some people who have suffered innocently have returned. You have to understand their position. But some of these people muddied the waters, rushed ahead of things, made themselves tiresome, and tried to confuse us. I'll tell you confidentially: Do you know what their slogan is? "Down with and hail!" Down with what, hail what? No one knows. The main thing is "down with," and afterward we'll see![35]

It was against this background of conflicting currents—tending, in one direction, to overflow the channel cut by Party criticism and, in the other, to turn back the flood—that a dramatic incident affecting the history of the war took place: An open dispute flared up between two major military organs about how the new data affecting Stalin's role in history, and the general revisionary spirit being sponsored by the Party, should be applied to the interpretation of the war. In April, *Military Herald* published an editorial that presented a far-reaching revision of the history of the war, bolder than anything ever aired before publicly.[36] Its main point was that the early defeats of the Soviet Army were due not to the surprise of the German attack, but to the negligence of the Soviet Government in failing to take the precautionary measures called for by elementary prudence and ample intelligence warnings. Included in this indictment was the charge, first made by Khrushchev in his secret speech, that the prewar industrial planning of the Soviet Union had not been properly geared to defense needs. Secondary points of the article ran a broad gamut of criticism tending to deprecate or even debunk the official historiography of the war. Included was an unprecedented criticism of the concept of the counteroffensive as it had been applied to the interpretation of the Stalingrad battle. From the accounts of this battle sponsored by official propaganda, *Military Herald* scornfully observed, the conclusion seemed justified that "it was fitting and even proper that Soviet troops should have retreated to Stalingrad, since this caused the enemy to 'expose' his flanks."[37] Finally, in an egregious understatement, which must have touched exposed political nerves, the editorial noted that there had been "a lack of proper attention to so important a question as the casualties and losses of material in various battles and operations."[38]

Shortly thereafter, on the anniversary of Victory Day, *Red Star,* the official organ of the Ministry of Defense, came out with a sharp rebuttal of these charges and a direct criticism of *Military Herald.* It was "surprised and grieved," it said, by the erroneous and harmful opinions contained in the *Military Herald* editorial. It described as "strange and unconvincing" its assertion that the defeats of the early period of the war were caused by the lack of preparedness of the Soviet armed forces. Moreover, it said, the question of the industrial preparedness of the country, as presented in *Military Herald,* was "grossly" distorted. The reasons for the reaction in *Red Star* were not hard to find. In the first place, it reflected the wounded vanity of the military chiefs—Zhukov in particular—who had shared some responsibility for the state of the nation's defenses on the eve of the war and who would inevitably share some of the blame for any mismanagement charged. Secondly, it reflected a concern, quite natural to the military establishment in the stormy atmosphere of the post–Twentieth Party Congress period, that the denigration of Stalin was being carried to the point where the moral basis of authority in the armed forces was being shaken. *Red Star* made this concern explicitly clear.

Our commanding personnel plays a decisive role in further strengthening the combat preparedness of our forces. Our commanders, who possess lofty moral and military qualities, very extensive experience from the last war, and good military and theoretical training, will carry out still more successfully the duties of military and political leaders of the troops—that is, carry out the duties of individual leaders, of direct organizers of a unified process of the training and upbringing of personnel. The Communist Party has pursued, and still pursues, the policy of further strengthening one-man command. It is quite clear that one-man command should not be confused with the cult of the individual, *as some politically immature people are inclined to do.*[39] [Italics added.]

While this drama was being played, *Questions of History* was imparting its own vigorous thrust to the revisionary movement. In its April issue, it published a directive article calling for a broad review of virtually the whole historical legacy of the Stalin era, including the history of the war.[40] In May, it published a more detailed attack on the past official history of the war, in the form of a critique by Major General E. A. Boltin of the *Essays on the History of the Great Patriotic War.*[41] This article supported and elaborated the main tenets of the *Military Herald* editorial, and also introduced an entirely new element into the revisionary movement—a call for a more appreciative evaluation of the contributions of the Allies in the war. The scope of revision proposed in this matter was conveyed by the author's specific criticisms of the *Essays*. These critical comments may be paraphrased as follows: The *Essays* had failed to show (1) the relationship between the Great Patriotic War and World War II; (2) the "liberational, antifascist character" of World War II even before the U.S.S.R. entered it; (3) the contribution made by the anti-Hitler coalition to the U.S.S.R.; (4) the "positive results" of the North African operations; (5) all the "military and political importance" of the Allied invasion of Europe; (6) the actions of "our partners in the anti-Hitler coalition" in the Pacific war. The author could well say, in line with the spirit expressed in these criticisms, that there was "the greatest historic importance in the fact that the Soviet socialist state . . . gained allies among the majority of these [capitalist] states in the war against world fascism."[42]

In the meantime, the issue raised by *Red Star*, which had remained unresolved for two months, was finally settled. In July, after the publication of the Central Committee document on overcoming the cult of personality, which indicated that the Party intended to continue the anti-Stalin campaign, the Party's theoretical organ, *Kommunist*, intervened to rebuke *Red Star* for its sally against *Military Herald*.[43] *Kommunist* went down the line in supporting all the main theses of the *Military Herald* editorial, including the delicate issue of the prewar industrial preparedness of the country. The shortages of equipment that developed in the early period of the war were the result, it admitted, of "a serious omission in the planned development of military industry in the prewar years."[44] It also endorsed, incidentally, in somewhat less enthusiastic language, the more positive approach to the role of the Allies in the war that *Questions of History* had supported.

On July 19, two days after this issue of *Kommunist* had gone to press, *Red Star* announced its capitulation on the issue of the pre-war preparedness of the country. But the capitulation was formal and qualified, for *Red Star* at the same time reiterated a defense of the military chiefs. It pointed out that the independent actions of other leaders, "including outstanding Soviet military commanders," had lessened the negative consequences of Stalin's personality cult. And it took pains to point out that among the matters distorted in the Stalinist histories of the war was "such an important factor as the role of the generals of the Soviet Army." The strong sense of corporate identity and pride reflected in these statements was expressed even more directly seven months later in Marshal Malinovskiy's Victory Day assertion that "the Supreme Soviet military command" had not been caught unawares by the German invasion. These statements throw a revealing light on prevailing attitudes in the army and add some substance to the Party's later charge that Zhukov had set the army apart from the Party.

July was the highpoint of the 1956 revisionary movement. In the following months it rapidly lost momentum. The nucleus of conservative opposition in the historical movement began to gain the upper hand in the fall. While the issues in the running battle concerned mainly internal Party history, the gradual ascendancy of the conservatives in effect placed the whole revisionist movement on the defensive. More important for the fortunes of the revisionist movement were the changes in the political climate in the latter half of 1956. The adverse political repercussions of the anti-Stalin campaign throughout the world undoubtedly exerted a depressing influence on the anti-Stalinist ardor of the Soviet leadership. When, at the end of October, the Hungarian revolt brought home with shattering impact the full depth of the crisis that had been created, the anti-Stalin campaign and all its attendant revisionary impulses were sharply curbed. For the next year or so, except for the regular anniversary observances, little more was heard about the revision of the history of the war in the Soviet Union, although the gains in historical realism of 1955 and 1956 were not renounced.

There remains to be considered the impact of these events of 1956 on the literary community.

The Literary Postlude

The literary community had reacted with its customary sensitivity to each development in the liberalization of Soviet policy after Stalin's death. The first flush of excitement evoked by the early cautious moves away from Stalin had produced the literary "thaw" of 1953–54, and the more far-reaching de-Stalinization of the Twentieth Party Congress produced the surge of literary activity that has been called the "year of truth" of 1956–57. Thoughts and aspirations bottled up for a decade were suddenly released in a series of literary works and declarations that brought the light of criticism to many dark corners of the Soviet system. The focus of the writers' attention was naturally the contemporary Soviet scene —the dry rot of the bureaucracy, the demoralization of Soviet man—the issues that would decide whether the writers' freedom to criticize and portray life as they saw it would be enlarged or curtailed. Yet the reforming impulse was broad enough to touch the Soviet past as well, and the history of the war was opened up to viewpoints not expressed before.

The enthusiasm for truth that the anti-Stalin campaign awakened in the writers' community was strikingly revealed by the public confessions of certain prominent Soviet writers of their guilt in permitting and assisting the falsification of the past. Konstantin Simonov made such a declaration in his article "Literary Notes," which appeared in December, 1956.[45] In his review of the postwar criticism of Fadeyev's *Young Guard,*[46] he commented bitterly on the weasel-worded accounts of the war in the official criticism at that time. He obviously considered the criticism of *The Young Guard* as typical of the whole postwar distortion of the history of the war, in which he had acquiesced. "Not everything went smoothly," he mimicked. "How can one speak thus of a war in which, by 1942, the fascists had occupied a territory having a population of almost 70 million?" Again mimicking the official formula, he quoted: "Various unforeseen circumstances arose." "What sort of wording is that? One can speak thus about a train being late, or about early frosts, but not about the war, the whole course of which from the very outset, to our great misfortune, was an unforeseen circumstance."[47] Alexei Surkov, the head of the Writers Union, spoke in the same vein. In the foreword to his *Old Field Notebook,* published in 1957, he admitted that during the early period of the war he had written falsely about the imaginary altruistic patriotism of the troops, concealing the defeatism that had actually prevailed in the army.[48]

These declarations, which indirectly testified to the weight of shame that the Stalinist past had imposed on Soviet consciences, expressed a common impulse of the literary works of this time. In one way or another, writers sought to expose and explain the demoralizing effects of the Stalinist tyranny, to probe the psychological roots of the moral passivity and political cowardice of Soviet man. The important works of the time, those that received the most critical notoriety in the Soviet press—Granin's "Personal Opinion," Yashin's "The Levers," Nagibin's "The Khazar Ornament" and "The Light in the Window," and others—all circled around this rankling theme.[49] Works on war themes were also affected by this preoccupation. It was the distinctive contribution the "year of truth" made to the literature of the war.

This revelatory spirit was displayed in two of the most substantial literary works on the war that appeared at this time: two stories by Simonov, which were parts of a projected novel. In the first of these, a short story entitled "Panteleyev," Simonov described an army division in which demoralization had set in from top to bottom.[50] At each command echelon, from the general on down to the company commanders, Simonov depicted disorder, confusion, even outright cowardice. "How could it happen," asked *Literary Gazette* in a subsequent angry review, "that in one division there appeared only cowardly commanders, cowards 'from top to bottom,' who 'feared causing failure more than the failure itself, feared responsibility for losses more than the losses themselves'?"[51] Simonov's answer, it appeared, was the same as that given in the other works of the period, that the tyranny of the Soviet system had dried up the springs of initiative and independence in the Soviet people. This answer was conveyed in his analysis of one of the officers involved in the story, a man who had been unjustly condemned, had spent two years in prison, and there "became frightened once and for all of life, became frightened of anything that anyone at any time could take it into his head to accuse him of."[52]

The problem of the moral condition of the Soviet system was approached from another angle in Simonov's second story, a novelette entitled "One More Day."[53] Here, in depicting a divisional political officer, he drew a picture of the demoralization that the bureaucratic life had wrought in the inner workings of the system itself. Every feature and mannerism of this officer, depicted in acid detail by Simonov, seemed to symbolize the decadence of bureaucracy: his bumbling unfamiliarity with such an elementary military skill as the doffing of his helmet; his faith in paper work, his "notebook"; his vindictiveness; his hypocritical secret drinking; his propaganda slogans; and, finally, his disbelief in Communism! This portrait, in addition to its symbolic significance, certainly also reflected a less abstract emotion—the antipathy of the front-line soldier for the rear-echelon, note-taking commissar.

Another story appearing at that time—"The Company Departs Singing," by Aleksandr Bylinov, for which Simonov, as the editor of the magazine in which it was published, bore some responsibility, presented characters just as unwholesome as the above-described officer.[54] It depicted a rear-area training regiment in which callous, incompetent officers permitted raw, half-trained recruits to be sent off to the front as cannon fodder. This situation, the story seemed to imply, was not due solely to the personal faults of the officers concerned, but to the whole system of supplying reinforcements to the front, which placed a premium on fulfilling the plan to the detriment of other considerations. As in "One More Day," political officers were portrayed negatively, and Bylinov, like Simonov, sarcastically drew attention to the symbols of the political worker's trade.

On the walls of the wooden camp structure there were painted in black such words as: "Soldier, stop the enemy! Stop and smash him! Smash and stop him!" "Not one step backward! Endurance is your life!" "Death to traitors, self-seekers, and cowards!" Daily the soldiers passed by these angry challenges on their way to their exercises in the field, to the mess hall, or to the hastily erected wooden clubhouse. The gigantic letters of the posters were carefully drawn everywhere possible by the regimental artist, Nikolai Savchuk, a former student in an art institute. He sketched multicolored canvases, pictures, and posters, and he covered the paths and streets of the camp with them, and also the walls of the buildings. He called all this, in the language of Shcherbak [the regimental commissar] "graphic agitation." "True," thought Arenskiy [an incompetent but honest officer], "these posters also help to train the soldier. But can they teach him to shoot?"[55]

In addition to these negative vignettes of military life, the literature of the time afforded occasional glimpses into some of the more sensitive secrets of the wartime past. The ferocity of Soviet military justice, which undoubtedly put steel into Soviet backbones during the war, but also scarred many memories, was for the first time displayed in a critical light in this literature. For example, the Bylinov story dealt with this subject from one viewpoint—the abuse of the organs of military justice by unworthy officials. It portrayed a neurotic prosecutor whose only interest in the case of the replacement regiment was to "broaden" the circle of the accused so as to win promotion for himself.

A more general viewpoint, which presented the military tribunals as a functional element in Soviet wartime discipline and

hinted at their fearsome and omnipresent power, was given in a
verse of Boris Slutskiy.

> Tired with the last fatigue,
> Seized by the death-before-death,
> His great hands limply spread,
> The soldier lies.
> He might be lying otherwise,
> He might be lying with his wife in his bed,
> He might not be tearing the blood-soaked moss,
> He might . . .
> Might he? Perhaps? If?
> No, it could not be otherwise.
> The Military Commissariat had sent him a notice,
> Alongside him the officers went, marching.
> In the rear, the tribunal's typewriter pounded.[56]

Finally, one other dark memory brought to light in literature by
the anti-Stalin campaign was the ruthless treatment meted out to
subject nationalities suspected of wartime collaboration with the
Germans. Belated tacit apologies for these crimes had already been
made in the course of the general overhauling of the Soviet legal
and penal system that began after Beria's arrest and execution. But
the airing of history that this involved was limited and grudging.
At the end of December, 1956, a more dramatic literary exposure
of this history was offered. The Latvian-language literary journal
Star published a poem entitled "The Unfinished Song," by Harijs
Heislers, which depicted the arrest and deportation to Siberia of a
young Latvian student after the reoccupation of Latvia by Soviet
troops.[57] The poem revealed the terror and personal suffering
caused by this injustice. Above the published poem appeared an
illustration showing a train of boxcars disappearing into an im-
mense, empty steppe, under a black and lowering sky.

The short-lived year of truth these works helped record produced unusual insights into Soviet attitudes toward the history of

the war. They showed that the postwar decade of official propaganda had been a failure in the one area in which it could have had genuine political significance—influencing the attitudes of the people toward the regime. Not only had it failed to erase the memories of the sufferings and sacrifices inflicted by the war, but it had added new resentments that the political self-centeredness and unfairness of the official historiography itself had engendered. True pictures of the war, as we have seen, had been given in Soviet literature before. But the bitter etchings of the post–Twentieth Party Congress period were quite different from the uninhibited accounts of the wartime years. Dudintsev once ascribed the anger he had expressed in his book *Not By Bread Alone* to the memory of frustrated impotence he had felt as he sought cover from the Messerschmitts flying unmolested in the Russian skies. Undoubtedly, such memories as these underlay the works of 1956–57 and imparted to them their peculiar aspect of a literary squaring of accounts.

7

The Consolidation of the
Post-Stalin Revisions

The need for a readjustment of the energizing impulses of the
Twentieth Party Congress to the more permanent goals and requirements of the Soviet system of power was evident to the Soviet
leadership after 1956. The post-Hungary reaction in the Soviet
official mood brought with it a reassertion of Party prerogatives in
the interpretation of history and a generally heavier ideological
hand in the exercise of these prerogatives. But as political self-
confidence gradually returned—particularly after the rout of the
anti-Party group in June, 1957, and the reaffirmation of Party
control over the armed forces with the ouster of Marshal Zhukov
in October, 1957—the regime resumed its active encouragement of
military history. New interpretations were worked out to adjust
the history of the war more adequately to the regime's image of
itself and the world around it. But within this political framework,
military historians were given greater freedom than ever before to
explore the military history of the war. World War II assumed a
place of prominence in Soviet history, and the flow of new books
on the subject soon surpassed the output of the past.

THE SHIFTING PROPAGANDA LINE

Signs of retrenchment in official attitudes toward the history of
the war began to appear by early 1957. The military chiefs, ap-

parently stung by the critical current they had helped to loose, were in the forefront of this reaction. Marshal Malinovskiy, in the major Armed Forces Day article of 1957, took a stand directly opposed to one charge of the revisionary historiography. "It must be said directly," he asserted, "that this [the German invasion] was not unexpected by the Supreme Soviet military command."[1] Marshal Meretskov departed even further from the spirit of 1956, sloughing over the early defeats and focusing attention on traditional inspirational themes. He even suggested a partial rehabilitation of Stalin: "This historic victory was achieved under the leadership of the Communist Party and its Central Committee headed by J. V. Stalin."[2] Marshal Moskalenko, writing in Red Star, barely mentioned World War II and said nothing about the early defeats.[3]

In general, there was very little press attention to the history of the war in the first half of 1957, perhaps less than during any comparable period since the end of the war. Contrary to past practice, ceremonial occasions, which used to draw attention to this subject, were passed by with few reminiscences. Even the Victory Day observances were muted, and Zhukov's Order of the Day and the accompanying editorials focused on the future rather than the past. The little that was written, moreover, was strongly defensive in tone. The Victory Day issue of Red Star was fairly typical of the Soviet press in this respect. It contained only one article on the war—a critique of Western "falsifications" of history—and only one allusion to the failures of the first period—an equivocal statement that "the socialist regime permitted our people . . . to overcome successfully the shortcomings in preparations for repelling the attack of the aggressors."[4]

The extreme caution of the propaganda in 1957 on this sensitive area of the Stalinist past reflected the profound disturbances that had been aroused within the leadership by the anti-Stalin campaign. It is now known that conservative elements in the ruling group had opposed Khrushchev's policy from the beginning. And as they collected evidence that the de-Stalinization campaign had weakened Soviet authority throughout the world Communist movement, Khrushchev's vulnerability to criticism increased. Not only had the personal reputations of powerful leaders been threatened, but the interests of the ruling group as a whole had now been placed in jeopardy. Brandishing this argument as a powerful weapon, the opposition to Khrushchev was in a position to stall any progress toward defining policy in this sphere. Thus, further developments affecting the history of the war had to await the resolution of this political conflict—a resolution that was effected by the purge of the anti-Party group in June, 1957.

Evidence of a stronger hand in the direction of World War II historiography was apparent from about mid-1957 on. The decision of the Central Committee in September to sponsor a new multivolume history of the war, and the creation of a special section in the Marxism-Leninism Institute to prepare it, marked a major turning point. This was followed by the ouster of Marshal Zhukov in October—an act that dramatized the supremacy of the Party over the military command.

The Party was at pains to emphasize, both in the resolution itself and in subsequent commentary, that the Zhukov ouster carried implications for the history of the war—implications that lay in details and emphases rather than in over-all policy. By tearing down the reputation of the army's most prominent officer, the Party reminded the historians that the Party alone was the arbiter of historical fortunes. However, its purpose was not to demean the army but to redefine the army's relationship with the Party. The army's role in history was to be given its due, but henceforth the role of the Party was to be shown in a light suitable to its newly asserted pre-eminence.

By the end of 1957, the official attitude toward the history of the war had become relatively stabilized. Having eliminated or tamed the internal political forces that could impede the adjustment it was seeking, the regime was now in a position to reach a settlement with its Stalinist past. The settlement was a compromise

—a solution that reflected the conflicting requirements the regime wished to impose upon history. For in seeking to reharness history to the goals and requirements of the Party, the regime did not wish to shackle the progress that was being made in the field of military thought—progress closely connected with and partly dependent upon the historical revisions of the past few years. Thus, the new Soviet line combined dual features: a concern to retain and develop the gains in military history achieved in 1955 and 1956, and a desire to bolster and refurbish the Party's historical reputation and ideological credentials.

Under the auspices of this political settlement, historical writing on the war flourished. Detailed studies of World War II military actions that had begun to appear as early as 1955–56 now began to assume a bulk and character that gave them independent significance as a gauge of official policy. These studies, largely sponsored by the Ministry of Defense, included accounts of small-unit actions in different types of operations, analyses of specific tactical problems, and unit and campaign histories.

The professional purposes underlying the publication of this literature were expressed in the foreword to a typical example brought out in 1958. Major General V. D. Vasilevskiy, the editor of a book entitled *Battle Operations of an Infantry Regiment,* explained the aims of the publication in the following way:

We must not underestimate the rich experience gained in the waging of battles, much less forget it. Despite the new weapon that has appeared at the present time, which, along with other factors, has had a great influence on our views regarding the conduct of battle operations in contemporary conditions, the experience of the Great Patriotic War has not lost its significance. The Great Patriotic War provided much that is instructive, which should be learned and reflected in organization and training and in the conduct of contemporary battles.[5]

The content of the book was also typical of this literature. It presented a collection of studies of individual infantry campaigns, providing exact data on the numbers of men and weapons involved. Each study was concluded by a brief critique of the shortcomings and failures displayed in the conduct of the action.

Even prior to 1957, another category of literature on the war had begun to appear on a substantial scale—translations of foreign works. The authors chosen for translation included German generals who had fought against the Soviet Union, Western military experts, and Western historians who dealt with particular aspects of the war remote from Soviet experience. Important documentary collections, such as the wartime correspondence of Roosevelt, Churchill, and Stalin and the records of the Nuremburg trials, also came out at this time.[6]

The scale of this publishing effort was attested to by the propaganda campaign against "bourgeois falsifications of history" that assumed a prominent place in the Soviet press after 1957. Ironically, most, if not all, of these criticisms were directed at works that had been translated and published in the Soviet Union. Thus, the criticisms reflected on the liberal publication policy that had permitted these books to appear. For example, two naval captains, writing in *Izvestia,* deplored the "incomprehensibly indulgent and careless attitude of our publishing houses toward such specimens of falsification of history."[7] Of the two publishing houses principally engaged in this activity—the Military Publishing House and the Publishing House of Foreign Literature—the latter came in for the sharpest barbs in this respect. It must be stressed, however, that these criticisms did not directly challenge the policy of publishing foreign literature. They complained only of the failure of editors and publishing houses to supply adequate critical forewords and footnotes.

The major index of the new, more settled policy toward the history of the war was the appearance of a number of general histories that provided integrated summations of the trends in policy and historiography described above. Two influences were primarily responsible for bringing these new histories to fruition. One was the

Central Committee decree of September, 1957, mentioned above. In addition to authorizing an official textbook, this decree had the effect of focusing the attention and efforts of the historical community on the subject of World War II history and of starting a race to exploit the newly opened market. The other was the patronage of the Ministry of Defense, whose interests in a restudy of World War II experience had from the beginning given the revisionary historiography its impetus and direction.

THE HISTORICAL ISSUES: CHANGE IN CONTINUITY

The comparison of the interpretations offered in these new histories with past interpretations of the same events throws light on the practical effects of these developments. In making these comparisons it may be useful to consider the military and political aspects of the war separately.

The Military Aspects

The charge that the Soviet Government was negligent in failing to prepare the military establishment for war—a charge first raised by Khrushchev in his secret speech and subsequently disputed by the military—has been retained, and greatly enlarged, in the current histories. In these accounts, Stalin is still presented as a culprit, but other figures are now made to share the dock with him. The first volume of the new official history of the war, published in 1960, asserts that "leading workers of the Peoples' Commissariat of Defense" did not appreciate the urgency of the moment, and were "impermissibly" slow in evaluating the designs of new weapons and equipment and in getting prototypes into production. In assigning blame, however, it restricts the list to secondary individuals: Deputy Commissars G. I. Kulik, L. Z. Mekhlis, and E. A. Shchadenko.[8] But the second volume of the same history, published in 1961, also includes Marshals Zhukov and Timoshenko in the indictment.[9]

The charge that Marshal Timoshenko shared responsibility for the initial unpreparedness of the Soviet Union and for the early defeats represented a major innovation in the Soviet history of the war. This was the first time his name figured directly in this connection, although the positions he had held during the early period of the war implicated him in the general charges of command failures during that period. He had been successively Peoples' Commissar of Defense, acting Commander in Chief of the Armed Forces, and Commander in Chief of the Western Direction during the most critical period of the war. Thus, whatever political reasons may have prompted the accusation, his vulnerability to historical criticism was beyond question.

The specific naming of Zhukov was itself unusual. In 1957, co-incident with his removal from the Central Committee, Marshal Konev had launched a violent attack on Zhukov's military reputation, charging him with responsibility for the poor state of the country's defenses. And the point had been brought up again in an authoritative article on the history of the war by Major General E. A. Boltin in 1958.[10] Surprisingly, however, despite the fact that Zhukov presented the classic qualifications for a scapegoat on this issue, the charge was not followed up until 1961. Moreover, it should be emphasized that even in the 1961 account the charge against Zhukov—as also the charge against Timoshenko—was presented more as a regretful observation than an indictment.

These and other accounts provide a revealing picture of the scale of disorganization in the Soviet military industry on the eve of the war. Only 17 per cent of Soviet aircraft in active status were of modern design;[11] the serial production of Yak-1's and Mig-3's (the first modern types) began only in 1941;[12] the rate of production of automatic weapons and machine guns actually decreased during 1940 and the first half of 1941;[13] the first antitank guns began to come out only in October, 1941.[14] And the list could be extended. One could suppose that these facts are presented to mitigate the discredit cast by the military defeats of the early period, but the Soviet accounts do not present the facts in this way, and this does not appear to be the purpose of the revelations.

The newer accounts of the initial German attack are also remarkably revealing and equally well furnished with factual credentials. The picture of Soviet military unpreparedness that had been drawn in previous German accounts of the war is now fully confirmed in the current Soviet histories. It has now been conceded— and corroborated with a wealth of detail—that border fortifications were not completed, that troops had not been placed on a war footing, that many divisions of the border screen were at reduced strength and others consisted of untrained contingents newly called up on the eve of the war, etc. These failures of military leadership, it is said, were compounded by political mistakes. To avoid giving the Germans any pretext for hostilities, most divisions of the border screen were ordered to keep only one of their regiments on the border, while the main forces were held in camps or military towns well behind the front.[15]

While always extolling the "staunchness" of the Soviet resistance to the German invasion, these accounts also provide many details that bring out the scale of the initial catastrophe. One account provides exact figures on the extent and tempo of the German advance. The same source freely acknowledges the ineffectiveness of Soviet resistance at particular junctures. For example: "Neither in the border area nor on the line of the western Dvina nor at the Pskov and Ostrovskiy fortified regions could the troops of the northwestern front hold back the adversary."[16] Or again: "The Command of the southwestern front was unable to organize the leadership of the military operations of the encircled troops. Direction of the troops was lost, and the withdrawal took place in an extremely disorganized manner, by separate groups and units."[17]

The time-honored doctrine of the "counteroffensive" appears to have fallen by the wayside in current historiography. The first volume of the new official history reveals that the problems involved in the counteroffensive had not even been raised in Soviet military theory before the war, thus clearly implying that the concept could not have affected the planning and conduct of operations during the early period. The same source states that defensive strategy as a whole was badly underdeveloped in Soviet military doctrine before the war. Soviet strategy, it declared, recognized defensive action as "possible and necessary" on individual sectors, "but not on a whole strategic front."[18]

Some flavor of the earlier descriptions of the counteroffensive is recreated in the second volume of the new history, where the actual course of operations during the early period is described. In terms reminiscent of the military theorists of the Stalinist period, the book describes the "task" that the course of events during the early period had posed for the Soviet armed forces, i.e.: "Through stubborn defensive battles to exhaust and bleed white the huge forces of the enemy and to stop him on the decisive spots. Only by fulfilling this task would it be possible to prepare and subsequently successfully carry out a decisive counteroffensive."[19] That this represents only a superficial recidivism of language, however, and not a genuine rehabilitation of the concept, is indicated by recent press and journal articles that clearly link the doctrine of the counteroffensive to the distortions of the "personality cult" era, thus seemingly insuring its final oblivion.

Changes have affected the presentation of a number of other military operations of the war. For example, the 1942 withdrawal operations leading up to the battle of Stalingrad had formerly been presented as a skillfully managed maneuver designed to set the conditions for a counteroffensive. The latest full history of this period, however, provides a clear picture of the forced character of the Soviet retreats during the summer of 1942. "The enemy," it says, "having a considerable superiority of forces, held the initiative completely, while the Soviet units withdrew ever further southward." And citing the German author Hans Doerr, it quotes: "In those days, the Soviet Union underwent a severe crisis. . . . To all appearances, the Russians, even though they had executed a planned withdrawal to the Don, were forced under the pressure of the German units to retreat to the Volga and to the Caucasus earlier than planned; in several sectors their retreat turned into flight." The Soviet author disputes Doerr's view that there had been a "crisis" and that the Soviet retreat had been geared to any timetable, but he does not take issue with the assertion that in spots the retreat had turned into flight and admits explicitly that the military situation had "sharply deteriorated."

The same source provides a vivid account of the disorganization that prevailed in the Soviet retreat toward the Caucasus before the southern thrust of the two-pronged German offensive of 1942.

There were no prepared defensive fieldworks on the left bank of the Don, and our troops, hurriedly assuming the defensive, were forced to repel the attacks of the enemy from unprepared positions. The artillery fell behind at the crossing of the Don, and the defending troops were virtually deprived of artillery support. Due to shortages of aircraft, the troops of the front received no air cover. The situation in the rear and the material-technical supply of the troops was bad. Severe shortages of munitions, gasoline, and food were caused by the cutting off of rear installations and bases and interruptions of the regular supplies to the troops. The roads were torn up by machines, carts, and herds of cattle that created jams and slowed down movement.[20]

Another long-held Soviet proposition affecting the interpretation of Stalingrad—the claim that the German strategic objective in the summer of 1942 was neither Stalingrad nor the Transcaucasus but Moscow, and that Stalingrad was simply a way-station in a vast, enveloping maneuver aimed at the Soviet capital—has also been discarded in current Soviet historiography. The first direct attack on this interpretation was launched by Marshal Eremenko in a commemorative article on the fifteenth anniversary of the battle of Stalingrad in *Kommunist,* No. 1, 1958. "Our former interpretation of the German Command's plans for the summer of 1942 . . ." he said, "was unjustified." The true intention, he as-

serted, was the seizure of the rich material resources of the Transcaucasus, and the operations against Stalingrad developed out of
the military needs of this strategy. While this correct historical
interpretation appears now to have been accepted in Soviet historiography, the old view is dying hard. Recent accounts adduce
writings by Marshal von Paulus (prepared after the war) that
give support—as they were undoubtedly intended to do—to
the original Soviet interpretation. According to Von Paulus' account, the ultimate objective of German strategy in the summer
of 1942 was indeed the envelopment of Moscow. He explains
the absence of any reference to such an objective in the German
operational directives of 1942 by the phased nature of the alleged
strategy. As events developed in 1942, it became clear that the
ultimate objective could not be undertaken until 1943. The *Military-Historical Journal,* in first presenting this account, introduced
it with the noncommittal statement: "In the interests of collating
different points of view relative to the plans of the German Command in 1942, it is not without interest. . . ."[21] Another source introduced it in a footnote without evaluative comment, retaining in
the text an accurate account of the German documents bearing
on the question.[22]

In addition to such major revaluations, there are other signs
that military historians are now taking a fresh look at the whole
history of World War II military operations. Areas of criticism
never broached before—evaluations of actual command decisions
as well as the actions of high military echelons and individual
officers—have now apparently been opened. Eremenko, for example, in the article referred to earlier, made an unprecedented criticism of a General Headquarters decision in connection with the
Stalingrad battle. General Tyulinov, in an article in the *Military-
Historical Journal* (which incidentally provides unusual insights
into command disorganization during the early days) included
a similar criticism. Complaining that a General Headquarters deci-

sion had prevented a timely withdrawal of his troops at a critical juncture of the war, he observed with some petulance:

If the withdrawal of the troops proposed by the Command of the Southern Front [his command] on July 28 was a necessary condition for preserving life, and might have been carried out [at that time] in a planned manner . . . it had become unavoidable, and had to be effected under the pressure of the enemy in a more complex and difficult situation, when the directive of General Headquarters to withdraw by August 10 was [finally] received on August 5.[23]

In another departure from past practice, Tyulinov recounted a wartime episode that reflected unfavorably on a fellow general, and a similar though less personally derogatory reference was contained in an article by Marshal Grechko in another issue of that journal.[24] Even highly esteemed living officers have experienced a mild taste of criticism. Both Eremenko and Chuykov have been included among writers criticized for historiographical shortcomings in the *Military-Historical Journal.*[25]

The Political Aspect

The trend noted in the military writings toward recognition of the utility of truth (or at least the liabilities of falsehood) cannot be viewed in isolation. Rather, it must be considered in the context of the reaffirmation conveyed in political writings that history must ultimately serve the objectives of the regime, and that it can best perform this service by reinforcing the regime's image of itself and of the world in which it operates. Accordingly, since late 1957, Soviet historians have been engaged in drafting a framework of interpretations designed to set the history of the war more firmly into this political *Weltanschauung.*

The initial and central question for Soviet history was the definition of the character of the war. In this as in so many other areas of the history of the war, the problem had been created by Stalin. In his electoral speech of 1946, he had declared that the war had assumed "from the very outset" the character of a war of liberation and that the entry of the Soviet Union had merely "strengthened" this character. The formula contained some pitfalls, however, which became evident as the postwar campaign of denunciation against the West brought with it a complete revaluation of Allied motives in the war and a renewed denigration of Allied prewar policies. A more fundamental difficulty with the formula was that it provided no respectable explanation for the role of the Soviet Union during the first two years of the war or for the Communist parties of Western Europe that had opposed the war until the Soviet Union entered it.

These problems were largely evaded during the Stalin period by treating the Soviet-German War as a distinct historical entity somehow separate from World War II as a whole. During the first years after Stalin's death, historians took recourse to the traditional Soviet propaganda distinction between the governments and "peoples" of the Western states—a device that permitted credits to be allotted for a Western contribution to the victory while leaving basically intact the hostile assessment of "imperialist" policies during the war. This solution was presented in the major historical work of that period, the *Essays on the History of the Great Patriotic War,* published in 1955. The struggle against fascism had been justified, it explained, because the fascists had set as their goal the establishment of world domination and the subjugation of other peoples. "This is why World War II, although caused by the struggle of two hostile imperialist groups, from the very beginning began to carry a liberational character for the peoples of those countries who had been attacked by the fascist aggressors or were threatened by such attack. The liberational, antifascist character of the war became still stronger when the Soviet Union later entered it."[26]

The formula was brought up for review, along with the rest of the Stalinist history of the war, in 1956. In his biting criticism of the *Essays on the History of the Great Patriotic War,* Major

General Boltin decried the failure of Soviet historiography to acknowledge the positive contributions of the Allies in the war, observing that as a result, the "thesis on the strengthening of the liberational, antifascist character of World War II is left hanging in the air."[27]

A more permanent solution began to emerge in 1957 in connection with preparations for the new multivolume history of the war called for by the Party's September, 1957 decree. A meeting organized by the editorial board of *Kommunist* at the time produced what the journal later described as "heated disputes on the character of World War II." According to *Kommunist,* the new section on the history of the war in the Marxism-Leninism Institute had undertaken a serious study of the problem, and a lively discussion had begun throughout the historical community.

The result of these deliberations was an elaborate general theory of the character of World War II, which was first presented in an article in *Kommunist* early in 1958.[28] The new theory, distinguished from the earlier formulas mainly by a greater elasticity and comprehensiveness, has held up well. Its essential points, drawn from a composite of *Kommunist*'s presentation and two subsequent ones,[29] may be briefly summarized as follows:

In the prewar years, the policies of the Western states were affected by two basic "contradictions" in the world balance of forces—the first stemming from the expansionist pressures of Germany, Italy, and Japan against the Versailles settlement, and the second from the rise of the Soviet Union heralding the birth of a new socio-economic order. Although the latter tended to deepen and exacerbate all the old conflicts within the capitalist system, it served also to unite the reactionary forces. Hoping to use Germany as a striking force against Communism, the Western states assisted in the buildup of German military power and directed their whole prewar policy toward instigating a war between Germany and the Soviet Union. But Hitler, not wishing to be used as a pawn, launched war first against his imperialist competitors. The response of the Western states to Hitler's attack on Poland was prompted by a desire to defend their imperialist positions. Hence, the war began as an imperialist war on both sides.

However, unlike World War I, which involved merely a redivision of markets and spheres of influence, World War II involved the very existence of states and the question of the further spread of fascist tyranny. Thus, opposition to Hitler took on the character of a liberational mission. The Western states did not share this mission during the first part of the war; instead of resisting Hitler, they settled down to a "phony" war, persisting in efforts to arrange a deal with him and plotting attacks on the Soviet Union from Finland and the south.

The "people," however, recognized the true nature of Hitlerism and began to struggle against it. "In the course of time," wrote *Kommunist,* "the gradual accumulation of elements of liberational struggle could not fail to influence, and did in fact influence, the character of World War II. Thanks to the active antifacist struggle of the popular masses of countries occupied by Germany and Italy . . . the war, which international imperialism had envisioned as a means of dividing the world, began, through the efforts of the popular masses, to turn into an antifascist, just war of liberation." This changing character of the war justified the change in the attitude of the Western Communist parties. Having correctly assessed the war as imperialist initially, the parties had opposed it. However, when the situation changed, the Communists "came out for a decisive prosecution of the war, for the unification of all forces able to rebuff the onslaught of the Hitlerites."

For individual countries, the character of the war changed at different times. In Poland, the struggle was just and liberational from the outset. In Britain, the change occurred (in May–June, 1940, according to the first two accounts) when the government, "forced" by the pressure of public opinion, and itself recognizing the peril of the moment, began to fight for the independence of

the country. In France, the change came with the rise of the resistance movement. For the United States, the war had already
become liberational when she entered, and hence, the American
contribution shared in the character of the general enterprise.
However, the nature of the bourgeois governments, the class character of their policies, did not change. Although the "objective consequences" of their opposition to Hitlerism were progressive,
their aims and motivations remained imperialist throughout.

The policy of the Soviet Union was based upon a correct assessment of the anti-Soviet intentions of the imperialist states. In their
conversations with the Soviet Union in 1939, the Western states
were merely attempting to disguise concurrent efforts to arrange an
alliance with Germany. The threat of a single imperialist bloc
against the Soviet Union was averted by the acceptance of the
German proposal for a nonaggression pact. By this "outstanding"
diplomatic victory, the Soviet Union struck a blow at imperialism,
strengthened the position of socialism and democracy throughout
the world, and won valuable time to prepare for war.

This, in general outline, is the framework of political interpretations in which the current Soviet history of the war is set. Its effect
has been to reinforce the traditional interpretations and to further
darken colors in which the history of the Allied part in the war
is presented.

The case against the United States, particularly, has been drawn
tighter. Three years ago, an account of the Munich negotiations
presented the Americans as merely sympathetic bystanders, shar-
ing the objectives of Chamberlain and Daladier, but unable to take
a direct hand in the affair. By contrast, the most recent official
history concludes its account with the words: "That was how the
governments of the United States, Britain, and France staged the
abominable farce."[30]

Finally, the newer accounts are beginning to carry a heavier
embroidery of facts—evidence that Soviet historians are beginning
to recognize a need for a more plausible presentation of historical

interpretations than has been given in the past. The treatment of
the Nazi-Soviet pact in the first volume of the new official history
is illustrative. First, the amount of space devoted to the episode—
four and a half pages of concentrated text—is in sharp contrast
to the past practice of skipping lightly over this affair. In three
recent general histories covering the period, for example, the pact
receives variously from two and a half pages in the longest account
to three sentences in the shortest.[31] More important, the new account is closely tied to a set of facts. For the first time in Soviet
history, to the author's knowledge, the Astakhov-Weizsäcker exchanges are acknowledged. The first contact is placed in May, and
the initiative is laid entirely to the German side. The course of
the negotiations is presented as a drama of ardent pursuit on the
part of the Germans and virtuous denial on the part of the Soviet
Union, with the latter defending its innocence to the last. But
despite the sanctimonious interpretation, some impression of the
thread of the negotiations is conveyed. And in quoting Astakhov's
report in mid-August that, in his opinion, the Germans were prepared to make declarations and gestures that "a half year earlier"
would appear to have been completely excluded, there was even
some hint of the murkier background of exchanges that preceded
the acknowledged ones. It must be emphasized, of course, that the
novelty of the presentation is one of form, not of substance. The
familiar rationalizations and justifications are offered. The Soviet
action is presented as a *pis aller* necessitated by the nature of the
last German offer. If it had been refused, war with Germany would
have become unavoidable. Its acceptance, however, brought many
favorable consequences and, to a large extent, "predetermined"
the ultimate victory.

THE ARMY'S ROLE IN THE NEW HISTORY

The progress that has been achieved in the historiography of
World War II in the Soviet Union can be ascribed in large part

to the influence of the military. Acting as a special interest group—enjoying influence at the highest levels of the regime, but dedicated to purposes distinct from those of the regime—the military has been in a position to exert constant pressure for historical revisions responsive to its own interests. If the Party supplied the spring for the revisionary movement in the history of the war, the military has supplied the spur.

The dominant role of the military in the new history of the war is evident from the historical activity it has sponsored. The Ministry of Defense has been the major patron of research and publication in this field. Books published by the Ministry of Defense—Platonov's *Second World War* (1958) and Kulish's *Second Front* (1960) may be mentioned as typical examples—are far superior in quality and objectivity to comparable books published by Party and academic publishing houses. The principal professional journal in this field, *Military-Historical Journal,* is published by the Ministry of Defense. This journal demonstrates a level of scholarship far above that of the average run of other Soviet academic journals.

Military historians themselves demonstrate awareness of the leading role they have been playing, and they give evidence of considerable impatience with the way in which the propagandists have handled the history of the war. The *Military-Historical Journal,* for example, gave a highly critical review of Tel'pukhovskiy's recent book, *The Great Patriotic War of the Soviet Union, 1941–45*—a typical example of the propagandistic literature that long dominated this field. Among the "multiplicity of facts and figures" provided by Tel'pukhovskiy, complained the review, "the main thing drowns—the military actions of the Soviet troops and their results. . . . Instead of instructive conclusions and generalizations, one gets only a collection of phrases and wordy discussions."[32]

A similar tone of professional impatience—coupled with what can only be interpreted as an overtone of soldierly resentment at the civilian rear echelons—is reflected in a review of Kiryayev's

The CPSU—Inspirer and Organizer of the Victory of the Soviet People in the Great Patriotic War. The main complaint of the review is that the book "underestimates" the events at the front. Conceding that the examples of labor heroism with which the book abounds are authentic, the review nevertheless points out that these examples are isolated from the surrounding circumstances— circumstances "that, strictly speaking, were created by the heroic feats of the soldiers."[33]

One senses in these remarks by military historians a hint of the deeper-lying tensions that surround the current Army-Party collaboration in the new history of the war. A classic portrayal of the antipathies generated by these tensions is contained in Nekrasov's *In the Trenches of Stalingrad.* Describing emotions that lie at a psychological level inaccessible to the corrective action of Party propaganda—that is, emotions that may be assumed to endure—Nekrasov's insights have permanent significance. He presents them in describing an episode in World War II.

The scene is a battalion command post just before the launching of an attack. The commander—the narrator of the story—is visited by a delegation from the "political department" that has come to observe the attack. The delegation includes two political officers, a regimental communications officer, and an officer from the divisional staff. In a transparent substitution of roles—dictated obviously by political discretion—Nekrasov presents the latter officer as the symbol of Party interference in military affairs. In every word and feature, the man epitomizes the alien intruder: the nonprofessional, officious outsider, whose identification is made unmistakable by the emblem of the political officer's trade—the ever-ready notebook. The substitution of roles is made the more obvious by the shadowy characterizations of the two ostensible political officers: depicted as "good lads," they move dumbly in the background, smiling inoffensively from time to time, eating canned rations, but otherwise contributing nothing to the scene but the representational significance of their presence.

As the scene opens, the divisional staff officer, a captain, is writing something in his notebook, wetting his pencil with his lips as he writes.

"You have thought through the course of the operation?" he asks, raising colorless eyes. He has long, front teeth that protrude over his lower lip.

"Yes, I have thought it through."

"The command attaches great significance to it. You know this?"

"I know."

"What about your flanks?"

"Flanks?"

"When you move forward, how will you cover your flanks?"

"I won't. The neighboring battalions will support me. I do not have enough people. We are taking a risk."

"This is bad."

"Certainly it is bad."

He writes something in his notebook.

"What resources do you have?"

"I have no resources but a handful of people. Fourteen men will go into the attack."

"Fourteen?"

"Yes, fourteen. And fourteen will remain on the line. Twenty-eight men in all."

"If I were in your place, I wouldn't do it that way."

He glances in his notebook. I can't take my eyes away from his teeth. Are they ever hidden, or do they always stick out like that? I slowly draw a cigarette case from my pocket.

"When you are in my place you can act as you like, but in the meantime allow me to act according to my own judgment."

He compresses his lips as much as his teeth permit him.[34]

The denouement comes when the battalion commander orders the visitors out of the command post. Nekrasov portrays the scene in such a way as to suggest the battalion commander's suspicion that his visitor is a coward. The divisional officer, characteristically, responds to the taunt with an implied threat of political reprisal. He suffers a final indignity as he catches his map-case on a nail at the door of the dugout and is forced to struggle with the obstruction before completing his graceless departure. The dialogue begins with the request of the battalion commander that all who are not taking a direct part in the operation leave the command post.

The eyes of the captain become round. He closes the newspaper.
"Why?"
"Because . . ."
"I ask you not to forget that you are talking to a superior."
"I forget nothing. I ask you to go from here. That is all."
"I interfere with you?"
"Yes. You interfere."
"In what way?"
"By your presence. The tobacco. You see what's happening here. It's impossible to breathe."
I feel that I am beginning to speak foolishly.
"My place is at the battalion observation post. I am supposed to follow your work."
"That means that you intend to be with me at all times?"
"Yes, I intend to."
"And you will attack the hill with me?"
For several seconds he looks at me fixedly, not blinking. Then he rises demonstratively, deliberately folds the newspaper, thrusts it into the map-case, and, turning to me, carefully choosing each word, he says:
"Very well. In another place we will speak."
Then he crawls into the slit trench. At the door he catches his map-case on a nail and for a long time cannot free it.[35]

It is in the light of this background that some of the compromises and adjustments embodied in the new history of the war should be viewed. For the army's stake in history was embodied not only in current practical needs but in a sense of corporate honor—in a determination to cleanse the army's record of the blemishes left by Stalin. This motive is sensed in one of a recent series of *Red Star* articles reviewing the history of the Soviet armed forces.[36] Recalling the beginning of World War II, the author takes pains to show that it was not the army that was at fault for the initial unpreparedness of the country. From 1938 to 1940, he points out, the troops received no fewer than twenty-six manuals embodying the most up-to-date instructions on current military problems. On the eve of the war, moreover, he adds, twelve more regulations were worked out. One is reminded of Marshal Malinovskiy's aggressive assertion in 1957 that the Supreme Soviet Military Command had not been caught unawares by the German attack.[37]

Party policy toward the army in recent years testifies to the continued relevance of this psychological problem. The Party moved quickly after the ouster of Marshal Zhukov to reassure the military's sense of professional pride. For the first time in history, it named a line officer to the sensitive post of head of the Main Political Administration. And its propaganda repeatedly stressed the point that the improvement of Party controls in the army would be sought in alliance with the officer, not in opposition to him.

The acknowledgments at the Twenty-Second Party Congress that the military purge trials of the 1930's had been based on fabricated evidence is the most recent example of the Party's responsiveness to the army's sense of corporate pride. For two decades, the army had borne the stigma of these trials—a holocaust that had cut down not only the army's most distinguished general officers but a large part of the professional officer corps as a whole. Khrushchev's digression to this episode at the Congress was the more remarkable in that it was the only statement he made that bore in any direct way on the history of World War II—a subject that had occupied a large part of his original indictment of Stalin. Thus, it seemed to represent his belated amends. For the army— which celebrated the event with a stream of articles in the military press recalling the careers of the rehabilitated victims—it was the correction of a rankling historical injustice.

Speaking of the purge trials some years after the event, the hero of Simonov's novel *The Living and the Dead* asked plaintively: "Why was it necessary to deprive the army of such people before this war?" Himself a reprieved victim of the purge, he feels that his life is henceforth hostage to "those who still remained." His goal is to prove by his example the "stupidity" of this crime.[38] It may be assumed that Simonov's hero is not untypical of the Soviet professional officer. To such men, the righting of historical wrongs affecting the history of the war would appear not as a quixotic goal but as a responsibility imposed by history.

Conclusions

The Soviet leadership showed a highly consistent attitude through-out the postwar period, both during Stalin's lifetime and after it, in approaching the history of the war as an instrument for influencing social attitudes rather than as a subject deserving truthful evaluation in its own right. Thus, the Soviet official interpretation of the war was like a mirror of the current policies of the regime, and it is necessary to examine the policies to understand the rationale of leadership attitudes in this sphere.

At the end of the war, the Soviet regime stood at a crossroads. Had it wished to do so, the Soviet Union could have created a more peaceful international atmosphere by exploiting the good will it enjoyed in the world to secure a satisfactory relationship with the Western states and mobilizing the war-awakened initiative of its own people to supply the energy for its internal reconstruction programs. It could, on the other hand, return to the path it had followed in the past, re-creating an atmosphere of tension to supply a rationale and a goad for aggressive and expansionist policies.

Stalin took the latter course. The rigor of his policies in all spheres of Soviet life was a measure of the drift the Soviet Union had taken during the war from its historical course of development. The interpretation of the war that Stalin created was designed to obliterate the traces of that deviation, to convince the Soviet people that nothing had occurred to justify a change in the past policies of the Soviet Union. Thus, the history of the war became a paean to Stalin's political and military genius, a testament to the wisdom of Party policies, an indictment of the perfidy of the capitalist world, a proof of the soundness of the Soviet system.

The Stalinist version of the war distorted the historical facts in at least four major respects:

1. It presented the catastrophic defeats of the first year of the war as preplanned and skillfully executed maneuvers designed to set the conditions for a successful counteroffensive.

2. It magnified the roles of Stalin and the Party in the achievement of victory and diminished the roles of the military leaders and the ordinary people.

3. It deprecated the contributions of the Allies and sought to transform their public image from partners in the anti-Hitler coalition into crypto-enemies of the Soviet Union and virtual allies of Hitler.

4. It exaggerated the significance of the Soviet role in the defeat of Japan.

After Stalin's death, the official interpretation of the war underwent important changes. The post-Stalin leadership found itself confronted by a political situation at home and a military-strategic situation in the world that required changes in Stalin's policies. The most important of these changes for the history of the war was a revised estimate of the likelihood and consequences of surprise attack in a future war. This revised estimate entailed a revision of the Stalinist history of the first period of the war in which the significance of surprise attack had been deprecated. Impetus toward a further revision of the history of the war was contributed by the Twentieth Party Congress. Khrushchev's secret speech, which portrayed Stalin as ignorant of military matters and as criminally responsible for the initial unpreparedness of the Soviet Union, lay the basis for removing the distortions connected with past exaggerations of Stalin's role. In addition, the general atmosphere of renovation stimulated by the Congress encouraged a more appreciative evaluation of the role of the Allies in the war.

In some respects, the post-Stalin leadership showed itself to be as limited and self-centered in its approach to the history of the war as its predecessor. It was guided purely by practical expedience in its corrections of history, and it was as reluctant as its predecessor to admit its own culpability for the mistakes made during the war. But the differences between the Stalin and post-Stalin regimes were as striking as the similarities, and perhaps even more significant. Stalin allowed the distortion of the history of the war to proceed to the point where vital state functions affecting the military preparedness of the country were adversely affected. The post-Stalin leadership showed itself to be fully alive to its responsibilities in these vital areas of government. It displayed a willingness to make hard decisions that went against the grain of long-established Soviet attitudes to fulfill these obligations.

During recent years, the regime has become more at ease with history. This does not mean that it is any less inclined than Stalin to regard history as an auxiliary of current propaganda, or that it is ready to concede even a partial autonomy to historical truth. But the present regime appears to be less dominated by the psychopathic fear of being mired in its own historical tracks. Having survived one crisis of a runaway historical rebellion caused by its politically inept revaluation of Stalin, it appears confident of its ability to control history in the future. It appears willing to keep history captive rather than execute it, as Stalin had done. In this spirit—and prodded by the army, which has had its own special reasons for wishing a revision of Stalinist history—the regime has sponsored an extensive historical activity that is now providing a genuine contribution to the history of World War II.

Varying degrees of resistance and opposition to the imposition of the official line during the postwar period were manifested by the professional military, the historians, and the writers. The character and intensity of these reactions differed with each group.

There was an evident appreciation among military officers of both the strengths and weaknesses of the Soviet military performance during the war, and a lack of enthusiasm for its idealization that had been encouraged by official propaganda. In at least one case, the military expressed clear and vigorous approval of an honest account of the war (and hence, implicitly, disapproval of the official view). A preference for facts over theory marked the professional military attitude toward the history of the war, an attitude that seemed to reflect a concern that the excessive idealization of military events would prevent a proper evaluation and application of the lessons they carried.

Historians demonstrated inertial resistance to the postwar propaganda assault on the West and its attendant historical distortions of the Allied role in the war, and before succumbing to official pressure in this regard gave indications of their disdain for the political considerations that motivated it. Like the military, the historians' reaction was based primarily on professional considerations. The undercurrent of tension between the historical community and the propaganda authorities, which was an unmistakable accompaniment of the historians' reaction to the official version of the war, was one sign of this professional orientation. In no case was there any indication that the behavior of the historians was motivated by political disaffection or by affinity for the West. Rather, it appeared to reflect a feeling, seemingly widely held in the historical community, that historical questions ought to be settled by historical criteria and by the historians themselves.

The writers demonstrated the most outspoken opposition to the official interpretation of the war. Again, as with the military and the historians, this opposition was based explicitly on the conflict of official demands with professional standards. Writers who remained true to their art were unwilling, and it seemed unable, to present what they conceived to be the grand and tragic epic of the war in the shallow terms of a political tract. In the ensuing clashes and demonstrations, it was evident that the inherent incompatibility between reality as artistically observed and reality as politically idealized could not be reconciled.

In gauging the significance of the resistance demonstrated by these professional and intellectual groups to the postwar propaganda line on the war, it is necessary to bear in mind the nature of the historical period in which this resistance was most clearly manifested. The first two or three postwar years were a time of perturbation and uncertainty, both in Soviet society as a whole and in the leadership itself. To many people, the official interpretation of the war, particularly during the earlier stages of its development, must also have seemed uncertain. It was developed in piecemeal fashion, was illustrative and indicative rather than exhaustive in nature, and left many issues open to question. Probably many of the phenomena of opposition were products either of a mistaken assumption that the interpretation of the war remained open to question or of confused ideas as to the scope and rigidity of the official line.

At the same time, there was evidence of an open, bitter, and angry opposition to the official line. The fact that indications of this opposition appeared at all in the Soviet press was a sign of the breadth and depth of the social attitudes it expressed. In Soviet conditions, a single expression of dissent must outweigh a hundred pages of the standard antiphonal responses with which the Soviet press is filled.

On balance, we must conclude that there was a resistance to the official line on the war during the postwar period that was consciously motivated, was recognized as a conscious resistance both by the regime and by those who voiced it, and was of sufficient scope to invite the vigorous corrective action of the regime.

The major implications of this study relate to the Soviet intellectuals and their relationships with the regime. The tensions that arose in this sphere were a product not only of personal resentments and of independent spirits but also of the schizophrenia of the system itself, which required its intellectuals and professional specialists to serve two masters. Wherever the claims of politics and the truths of science and art remained unreconciled, tensions between these groups and the regime became apparent.

Finally, there is a moral aspect to the behavior of the Soviet intellectuals, an indication of the personal, secret conscience they maintained behind the façade of their public personalities. Throughout the ten years of the postwar period, and despite the powerful instruments of persuasion arrayed against them, they retained a strong resentment of the falseness and injustice of the Stalinist version of the war. This fact, this hardiness of the sense of truth and justice in an environment in which truth and justice tend to become expedient values, has relevance for us in the West. It is not in any sense a political fact that has immediate meaning. It is more important. It is a moral fact that attests to the validity of our faith and the prospects it opens up, that man does not live by bread alone.

Notes

Introduction

1. Konstantin Simonov, *Zhivyye i mertvyye* (Moscow, 1960), p. 70.
2. *Ibid.*, pp. 36–37.

Chapter 1—The Historical Issues and the Wartime Record
(pp. 3–36)

1. Weizsäcker memorandum, April 17, 1939, quoted in Raymond J. Sontag and James S. Beddie (eds.), *Nazi-Soviet Relations, 1939–1941* (Washington, 1948), pp. 1–2
2. S. P. Platonov (ed.), *Vtoraya mirovaya voyna, 1939–1945 gg.: voyenno-istoricheskiy ocherk* (Moscow, 1958), p. 163.
3. *Ibid.*, p. 176.
4. Winston S. Churchill, *The Grand Alliance* (Boston, 1951), pp. 358–61.
5. *Ibid.*, p. 367.
6. Raymond L. Garthoff, *Soviet Military Doctrine* (Chicago, 1953), p. 434.
7. Boris I. Nicolaevsky (ed.), "The Crimes of the Stalin Era; Special Report to the 20th Congress of the Communist Party of the Soviet Union, by Nikita S. Khrushchev," *New Leader,* Supplement, 1956, pp. 36–39.
8. Platonov, *op. cit.*, pp. 177–79.
9. Heinz Guderian, *Panzer Leader* (New York, 1952), p. 153.
10. Platonov, *op. cit.*, p. 179.
11. Erich von Manstein, *Lost Victories* (Chicago, 1958), p. 184.
12. J. F. C. Fuller, *The Second World War, 1939–1945: A Strategical and Tactical History* (New York, 1949), p. 124.
13. Platonov, *op. cit.*, pp. 219–20.
14. B. S. Tel'pukhovskiy *et al.* (eds.), *Ocherki istorii velikoy otechestvennoy voyny sovetskogo soyuza, 1941–1945 gg.* (Moscow, 1955), p. 104.
15. *Information Bulletin,* No. 4, July 18, 1941 (Embassy of the U.S.S.R., Washington, D.C.).
16. Leon Gouré, "Moscow in Crisis," in H. S. Dinerstein and Leon Gouré, *Two Studies in Soviet Controls: Communism and the Russian Peasant; Moscow in Crisis.* (Chicago, Ill., 1955).

17. Garthoff, *op. cit.*, pp. 425–26.
18. S. Borisov, "How the Leningrad Offensive Was Held," in *Strategy and Tactics of the Soviet-German War* (London, 1942), p. 48.
19. *The Great Patriotic War of the Soviet Union* (New York, 1945), p. 52.
20. E. A. Boltin, *Information Bulletin*, No. 28, August 15, 1941 (Embassy of the U.S.S.R., Washington, D.C.).
21. E. A. Shilovskiy, *Razgrom nemetskikh voysk pod Moskvoy* (Moscow, 1943), p. 19. A somewhat similar statement by Stalin, often quoted in later accounts, made the German miscalculation more general, and deriving also from the strength of the Soviet rear, the morale of the people, etc.
22. *Ibid.*
23. *Ibid.*, p. 25. For other contemporary references to German difficulties with the weather, see: I. I. Mints, "Razgrom nemtsev pod Moskvoy v 1941 g.," *Pravda*, December 6, 1942, and *Strategy and Tactics of the Soviet-German War*, pp. 40, 45.
24. *The Great Patriotic War of the Soviet Union*, pp. 14, 37, 53.
25. *War Speeches* (London, 1946), p. 139.
26. Fuller, *op. cit.*, p. 253.
27. Nicolaevsky, *op. cit.*, p. 41.
28. *Ibid.*, p. 40.
29. Churchill, *op. cit.*, p. 463.
30. Walter B. Kerr, *The Russian Army: Its Men, Its Leaders, Its Battles* (New York, 1944), p. 23.
31. *Ibid.*, p. 42.
32. *Ibid.*, p. 29.
33. Shilovskiy, *op. cit.*, p. 29.
34. Capt. N. Galay, "The Partisan Forces," in B. H. Liddell Hart (ed.), *The Soviet Army* (New York, 1956), pp. 153–71.
35. *War Speeches*, p. 139.
36. Kerr, *op. cit.*, p. 234.
37. John R. Deane, *The Strange Alliance*, quoted in Department of Military Art and Engineering, The United States Military Academy, *The War in Eastern Europe (June 1941–May 1945)* (West Point, N.Y., 1952), p. 118.
38. Guderian, *op. cit.*, p. 333.
39. *Voprosy Istorii*, No. 6, 1948, p. 137.
40. *Falsificators of History (an historical note)* (Moscow, 1948), pp. 10–12.
41. V. P. Potemkin *et al.* (eds.), *Istoriya diplomatii* (Moscow, 1945), III.
42. *Ibid.*, p. 654.
43. *Ibid.*, p. 647.
44. Frederick C. Barghoorn, *The Soviet Image of the United States* (New York, 1950), pp. 56–57.
45. Churchill, *The Hinge of Fate* (Boston, 1951), p. 341.
46. *Ibid.*, p. 342.
47. Barghoorn, *op. cit.*, p. 52.
48. *War Speeches*, pp. 95–96.

49. Barghoorn, *op. cit.*, p. 84.
50. U.S. Department of Defense, *The Entry of the Soviet Union into the War Against Japan: Military Plans 1941–1945* (Washington, 1955), pp. 52–53.
51. Todshikazu Kasé, *Journey to the Missouri* (New Haven, 1949), pp. 187–88.
52. *Ibid.*, pp. 193–94, 205.
53. *The Entry of the Soviet Union into the War*, p. 94.
54. *Ibid.*, p. 92.
55. Tel'pukhovskiy, *op. cit.*, p. 503.
56. *United States Strategic Bombing Survey: Japan's Struggle to End the War* (Washington, 1946), p. 13.
57. Kasé, *op. cit.*, p. 217.
58. V. Ya. Avarin, *Bor'ba za Tikhiy okean: agressiya SShA i Anglii, ikh protivorechiya i osvoboditel'naya bor'ba narodov* (Moscow, 1952), pp. 308–13.
59. Max Beloff, *Soviet Policy in the Far East, 1944–1951* (Oxford, 1953), p. 105.
60. *New Times*, September 1, 1945, pp. 9–11.
61. *Ibid.*, pp. 12–17.

Chapter 2—The Development of the Postwar Official Line
(pp. 37–63)

1. V. Pomerantsev, "Iskrennost' v literature," *Novyy Mir*, No. 12, 1953.
2. For Smith's protest and Molotov's curt rejection, see *Pravda*, October 1, 1947.
3. "Speech Delivered by J. V. Stalin at a Meeting of Voters of the Stalin Electoral Area of Moscow, February 9, 1946," *Information Bulletin*, March, 1946 (Embassy of the U.S.S.R., Washington, D.C.), p. 8.
4. *Pravda*, February 24, 1946.
5. *Ibid.*, May 9, 1946.
6. *Ibid.*
7. *Ibid.*
8. *Ibid.*, June 22, 1946.
9. Cited in Lt. Gen. P. Yarchevskiy, "Kontrataki, kontrudary, kontrnastupleniye," *Voyennaya Mysl'*, No. 3, 1947, p. 44.
10. *The Great Patriotic War of the Soviet Union* (New York, 1945), p. 52.
11. *Pravda*, June 22, 1946.
12. *Ibid.*, May 9, 1947.
13. *Ibid.*, June 22, 1947.
14. *Ibid.*, February 23, 1948.
15. "Speech Delivered by J. V. Stalin at a Meeting of Voters," p. 3.
16. *Iosif Vissarionovich Stalin, Kratkaya biografiya* (2nd ed.; Moscow, 1946), cited in Frederick C. Barghoorn, *op. cit.*, p. 149.
17. M. Galaktionov, *Pravda*, February 23, 1948. For the hardening of Soviet views regarding the American role in delaying the second front,

see the review of Ralph Ingersoll's book *Top Secret* in *Bolshevik*, No. 2, 1947. This review by the prominent propagandist D. Zaslavskiy placed strong emphasis on the alleged influence of American "reactionary circles" on this event. By contrast, the Soviet literary journal *Oktyabr'* treated this book quite differently in 1946. Excerpts from the book of Ingersoll, who was a former editor of *PM* and a staff officer at SHAPE during the war, had been serialized in *Oktyabr'* in the fall of 1946. The *Oktyabr'* commentary pointed out the conflicts between American and British staffs and emphasized British responsibility for delays.

18. I. I. Mints, *Otechestvennaya voyna sovetskogo soyuza* (Moscow, 1947).
19. *Ibid.*, p. 19.
20. *Ibid.*, p. 24.
21. *Ibid.*, p. 36.
22. *Ibid.*, p. 21. For contrast, see I. V. Anisimov and C. V. Kuzmin, *Velikaya otechestvannaya voyna sovetskogo soyuza, 1941–1945 gg.* (Moscow, 1952), a much more extensive work, which contains only this terse reference to the decree: "The State Defense Committee . . . calls all workers of the capital to observe order and quiet and to render the Red Army defending Moscow all possible cooperation."
23. *Ibid.*, p. 57.
24. *Ibid.*, p. 70.
25. *Ibid.*, pp. 27–28.
26. *Ibid.*, pp. 16–18.
27. *Ibid.*, p. 12.
28. *Velikaya otechestvennaya voyna sovetskogo soyuza. Materially po chetvertoy teme* (Moscow, 1948).
29. *Ibid.*, p. 8.
30. *Voprosy Istorii*, No. 6, 1951, p. 16. The articles by Voroshilov and Bulganin appeared in *Bolshevik*, No. 24, 1949.
31. N. Lapin, "Anglo-Amerikanskiye fal'sifikatory istorii vtoroy mirovoy voyny," *Voprosy Istorii*, No. 5, 1950.
32. *Ibid.*, p. 48.
33. Col. M. P. Tol'chenov, *Amerikano-angliskiye fal'sifikatory istorii vtoroy mirovoy voyny* (Moscow, 1953), p. 26.
34. *Voprosy Istorii*, No. 2, 1947.
35. *Ibid.*, p. 7.
36. *Voprosy Istorii*, No. 2, 1948.
37. Tel'pukhovskiy, *loc. cit.*, p. 35.
38. *Bolshevik*, No. 24, 1949, p. 43.
39. *Ibid.*, p. 68.
40. *Pravda*, October 10, 1952.
41. S. Kozhukhov, "K voprosu ob otsenke roli M. I. Kutuzova v otechestvennoy voyne 1812 goda," *Bolshevik*, No. 15, 1951.
42. *Ibid.*, p. 34.
43. "Pismo v redaktsiyu Zhurnala 'Bolshevik,'" *Bolshevik*, No. 19, 1951, pp. 71–72.
44. "Ot redaktsii zhurnala 'Bolshevik,'" *ibid.*, p. 78.

45. "Mikhail Illarionovich Kutuzov—polkovodeu *i* diplomat," *Voprosy Istorii*, No. 3, 1952, p. 34.
46. *Ibid.*, p. 35.
47. *Ibid.*, p. 37.
48. *VOKS Bulletin*, No. 54, 1948, p. 36.
49. *Kul'tura i Zhizn'*, November 30, 1947; *Pravda*, December 3, 1947.
50. See, for example, *Pravda*, January 16 and 17, 1950, for criticism of Katayev's *Za vlast' sovetov,* and *Pravda*, February 13, 1953, for criticism of Grossman's *Za pravoe delo*.
51. "Literaturnyye zametki," *Novyy Mir*, No. 12, 1956, p. 247.
52. *Falsificators of History* (Moscow, 1948).
53. U.S.S.R. Ministry of Foreign Affairs, *Documents and Materials Relating to the Eve of the Second World War* (New York, 1948).
54. *Falsificators of History*, p. 24.
55. *Ibid.*, p. 28.
56. *Ibid.*, p. 18.
57. *Ibid.*
58. *Ibid.*, p. 19.
59. *Ibid.*
60. Alexander Dallin, "The Month of Decision: German-Soviet Diplomacy July 22–August 22, 1939," *Journal of Central European Affairs*, IX, April, 1949, 6–7.
61. *Falsificators of History*, p. 22.
62. Quoted in *ibid.*, p. 24.
63. *Ibid.*, p. 17.

Chapter 3—The Military and the Interpretation of the War
(pp. 64–78)

1. See, for example, the discussion of the character of contemporary battles in *Voyennaya Mysl'*, No. 2, 1941, pp. 72–86.
2. "Dve strategii," *Voyennaya Mysl'*, No. 2-3, 1943.
3. *VOKS Bulletin*, Nos. 5, 6, 7–8, 9–10 (1945). Major General Galaktionov was one of the most prominent military theoreticians during the war and early postwar periods. In addition to writing for *Voyennaya Mysl'*, he contributed to *Znamya, Krasnaya Zvezda,* and *Pravda*. He was a member of the delegation of Soviet journalists that visited the United States in 1946. His death was announced in *Pravda*, April 5, 1948.
4. *VOKS Bulletin*, No. 5, 1945, p. 23.
5. *Ibid.*, No. 9–10, p. 10.
6. *Voyennaya Mysl'*, No. 6, 1946.
7. *Ibid.*, p. 4.
8. *Ibid.*, p. 5.
9. *Ibid.*, p. 6.
10. *Ibid.*, p. 16.
11. *Ibid.*, No. 6–7, 1945, p. 93.
12. *Ibid.*, p. 111.

188   NOTES

13. *Ibid.*, No. 8, 1946, p. 55.
14. In his article of repentance in *Voprosy Istorii*, No. 5, 1952, Tarlé pointedly noted that in his revised work he would take into account the two recent books on Kutuzov prepared by the military historians Lt. Colonel P. A. Zhilin (*Kontrnastupleniye Kutuzova v 1812 gody*), and Lt. Colonel L. Beskrovnyy (*Otechestvennaya Voyna 1812 gody i kontrnastupleniye Kutuzova*). The best bibliograpical guide to this whole subject was prepared by Colonel Meshcheryakov and appeared in *Voyennaya Mysl'*, No. 12, 1952, p. 70.
15. *Voyennaya Mysl'*, No. 4–5, 1945, p. 10.
16. For examples of relative objectivity, see Major Yezhov's discussion of the last phase of operations in the West in *Voyennaya Mysl'*, No. 6–7, 1945, p. 130, written in a detached style, although emphasizing throughout the debt of the Allies to the Red Army for their successes; also Major General N. Solodovnik's appraisal of the operational art and organization of the American Army, *ibid.*, p. 136, which was implicitly appreciative of the offensive-mindedness and practicality of the American Army. For an example of a stiffer attitude toward the Allies, see the editorial footnotes to the review of General Marshall's report, *ibid.*, No. 5, 1946, p. 64.
17. *Ibid.*, No. 3, 1955, p. 5.
18. Cf. Major I. Parotkin, "Organizatsiya proryva," *ibid.*, No. 6, 1942, and Col. A. Goncharov, "Tankovyye chasti v oboronitel'nom boyu," *ibid.*, No. 4, 1944.
19. *Voyennaya Mysl'*, No. 7, 1943.
20. *Ibid.*, pp. 5–6.
21. *Ibid.*, p. 6.
22. *Ibid.*
23. *Ibid.*
24. *Ibid.*, p. 7.
25. *Ibid.*, No. 6, 1942.
26. *Ibid.*, p. 18.
27. *Ibid.*
28. *Ibid.*, p. 22.
29. Shilovskiy, *loc. cit.*, p. 9.
30. "Zhurnaly rodov voysk i voprosy vzaimodeystviya," *Voyennaya Mysl'*, No. 6–7, 1945.
31. *Ibid.*, p. 166.
32. *Ibid.*, p. 167.
33. An analysis of Rotmistrov's article, which appeared in *ibid.*, No. 8, 1946, is given in Raymond L. Garthoff, *op. cit.*, pp. 312–14. Garthoff also notes how artillery proponents used certain of Stalin's statements to promote the claims of their own service. *Ibid.*, p. 302.
34. *Voyennaya Mysl'*, No. 6–7, 1945.
35. Although Penchevskiy's article was aimed specifically at an article by P. Yarchevskiy in *ibid.*, No. 4–5, 1945, he was undoubtedly aware that Galaktionov, in his article "Strategic Objective," had used the concept in the sense discussed in the text. Penchevskiy is not known

as an author in the field of military theory. This would suggest that he was a regular line or staff officer rather than a theoretician. Yarchevskiy, on the other hand, was a prominent theoretician, and his contributions include the first identification of the "counterblow" as a form of operations distinct from the counterattack and the counteroffensive. Cf. his "Kontrataki, kontrudary, kontrnastupleniye," *ibid.*, No. 3, 1947.
36. *Ibid.*, p. 67.
37. *Ibid.*, No. 3, 1949. Eremenko has had one of the most distinguished careers among Soviet general officers. He was commander of the Stalingrad Front during the battle of Stalingrad (where Khrushchev was his political opposite number). Subsequently, he commanded the 2nd Baltic Front and the detached Maritime Army in the Crimea, and at the end of the war was commander of the 4th Ukrainian Front. In 1955, he was promoted to Marshal of the Soviet Union, the highest military rank.
38. *Ibid.*, No. 3, 1949, p. 41.
39. *Ibid.*, p. 42.
40. "Nekotorye voprosy kontrnastupleniya po opytu velikoy otechestvennoy voyny," *ibid.*, No. 2, 1951, p. 40.

Chapter 4—The Professional Historians and the War
(pp. 79–102)

1. *Istoricheskiy Zhurnal,* No. 3, 1945, p. 60.
2. *Ibid.*, p. 64.
3. *Ibid.*, p. 63.
4. *Voprosy Istorii,* No. 4, 1946, pp. 146–49.
5. *Ibid.*, No. 3, 1947, p. 79.
6. *Ibid.*, No. 5, 1947, p. 168.
7. *Ibid.*, No. 5, 1953, p. 106.
8. *Ibid.*, No. 5, 1947.
9. *Ibid.*, p. 63.
10. *Ibid.*, p. 70.
11. "Napadeniye Yaponii na Pirl-Kharbor i nachalo voyny na Tikhom okeane," *ibid.*, No. 6, 1947.
12. *Ibid.*, No. 4, 1948.
13. *Ibid.*, p. 91.
14. *Ibid.*, No. 9, 1948, pp. 124–28.
15. Avarin, *Bor'ba za Tikhiy okean; Yapono-Amerikanskiye protivorechiya* (Moscow, 1947).
16. *Ibid.*, p. 243.
17. *Ibid.*, p. 352.
18. Beloff, *op. cit.*, p. 51.
19. Avarin, *Bor'ba za Tikhiy okean* (1947), pp. 403–4.
20. Avarin, *Bor'ba za Tikhiy okean* (1952).
21. The substance of this argument has been given in Chapter 1 of this work.
22. V. Lan, *SShA ot pervoy do vtoroy mirovoy voyny* (Moscow, 1947).
23. *Ibid.*, p. 203.

24. *Ibid.*, p. 151.
25. *Ibid.*, pp. 463–64.
26. *Ibid.*, p. 472.
27. *Trudy po novoy i noveyshey istorii* (Moscow, 1948), I.
28. *Ibid.*, p. 262. Source cited as *The New Statesman and Nation*, No. 398, 1938, pp. 518–19.
29. *Ibid.*, p. 249.
30. *Ibid.*, p. 254.
31. G. A. Deborin, *Mezhdunarodnyye otnosheniya i vneshnyaya politika SSSR 1917–1945.* Vypusk 4: *Gody velikoy otechestvennoy voyny* (Moscow, 1947).
32. *Kul'tura i Zhizn'*, August 21, 1949.
33. "Iz istorii Amerikano-Meksikanskikh otnosheniy v 1920–1939 godakh," *Voprosy Istorii*, No. 10, 1946.
34. "Politika soyedinennykh shtatov v Kube (1900–1934 gg.), *ibid.*, No. 11, 1947.
35. *Trudy po novoy i noveyshey istorii*, I, 163.
36. *Noveyshaya istoriya, 1918–1939 gg.* (Moscow, 1948).
37. *Ibid.*, p. 691.
38. *Ibid.*, p. 697.
39. *Voprosy Istorii*, No. 2, 1949, p. 156.
40. *Ibid.*, No. 5–6, 1946.
41. *Ibid.*, No. 10, 1947, pp. 158–59.
42. *Ibid.*, No. 2, 1948, p. 89.
43. Mints, "Lenin i razvitiye sovetskoy istoricheskoy nauki," *ibid.*, No. 1, 1949.
44. *Ibid.*, p. 14.
45. *Ibid.*, No. 6, 1948, p. 130; *ibid.*, No. 2, 1949, pp. 6, 155.
46. *Ibid.*, No. 3, 1948, p. 151.
47. *Ibid.*, No. 4, 1948, p. 146.
48. *Ibid.*, No. 12, 1948, p. 176.
49. *Ibid.*, No. 6, 1948, p. 139.
50. *Ibid.*, No. 11, 1948, p. 148.
51. *Ibid.*, p. 144.
52. *Ibid.*, No. 12, 1948, p. 177.
53. *Ibid.*, No. 6, 1948, p. 132.
54. *Ibid.*, p. 133.
55. *Ibid.*, No. 11, 1948, p. 147; *ibid.*, No. 12, 1948, p. 5.
56. *Ibid.*, No. 12, 1948, p. 12.
57. *Ibid.*, p. 5.

Chapter 5—The Writers and the War
(pp. 103–127)

1. Konstantin Simonov, *Days and Nights*, trans. Joseph Barnes (New York, 1945).
2. *Ibid.*, p. 159.
3. Vasiliy Grossman, *The Years of the War* (Moscow, 1946), p. 247.

4. *Ibid.*, p. 229.
5. *Ibid.*, p. 9.
6. Vasiliy Grossman, "The Stalingrad Offensive," in *Stalingrad* (Moscow, 1943), p. 132.
7. Grossman, *The Years of the War*, p. 263.
8. P. Vershigora, *Men with a Clear Conscience* (Moscow, 1949), p. 13.
9. *Ibid.*, p. 12.
10. Grossman, *The Years of the War*, p. 161.
11. *Ibid.*, p. 168.
12. Simonov, *Days and Nights*, p. 83.
13. "O cherepkakh i cherepushkakh," *Oktyabr'*, No. 5, 1946. I owe the felicitous translation of the title of Panferov's article to Vera Alexandrova, who offered it in her article "The Russian People and the 'Lost Peace'—in Literature," *Modern Review*, No. 7–8, 1949, which deals with much of the material considered in this chapter.
14. *Literaturnaya Gazeta*, December 22, 1945.
15. A. Volozhanin, "Pisatel' geroicheskoy temy," *Oktyabr'*, No. 3–4, 1946.
16. Panferov, *loc. cit.*, pp. 152–53.
17. *Ibid.*, p. 153.
18. *Ibid.*, pp. 154–55.
19. *Ibid.*, p. 159.
20. "Po povodu odnoy polemiki," *Literaturnaya Gazeta*, June 22, 1946.
21. "Rodina i Chuzhbina; stranitsy zapisnoy knizhki," *Znamya*, Nos. 11, 12, 1947.
22. *Znamya*, No. 11, 1947, pp. 132–35.
23. *Ibid.*, pp. 125–26.
24. *Ibid.*, p. 123.
25. *Ibid.*, pp. 120–21.
26. *Ibid.*, No. 12, p. 86. The Russian word I have translated as "grunt" is the onomatopoeic "khekat."
27. V. Ermilov, "Fal'shivaya proza," *Literaturnaya Gazeta*, December 20, 1947.
28. *Literaturnaya Gazeta*, December 27, 1947.
29. *Ibid.*, February 11, 1948. The case of Arkhipov provides an instructive example of the consistency and stubbornness with which young, independent-minded intellectuals retained their character throughout the repressions of the Stalinist era. He is almost certainly the same V. Arkhipov who, ten years later, ridiculed the officially approved novel *Bitva v puti,* by Galina Nikolayeva (*Neva*, No. 1, 1958), and was again attacked for his impudence by the official critics (*Kommunist*, No. 4, 1958).
30. "Teplokhod 'Kakhetia'; Zapiski voyennogo vracha," *Znamya*, Nos. 1, 2, 1948.
31. *Znamya*, No. 1, 1948, p. 5.
32. *Ibid.*, pp. 28–29.
33. *Ibid.*, p. 72.
34. *Ibid.*, p. 21.
35. *Literaturnaya Gazeta*, March 13, 1948.

36. "O 'zapiskakh' Ol'ga Dzhigurda," *Zvezda*, No. 4, 1948.
37. *Literaturnaya Gazeta*, May 8, 1948.
38. Vershigora, "O 'byvalykh lyudyakh' i ikh kritikakh," *Zvezda*, No. 6, 1948, p. 105.
39. *Ibid.*, p. 106.
40. *Ibid.*, pp. 106–7.
41. *Ibid.*, p. 108.
42. Pomerantsev's article appeared in *Novyy Mir*, No. 12, 1953. The resolution of the Presidium of the Board of the Union of Writers relieving Tvardovskiy as editor of *Novyy Mir* and appointing Simonov in his place was reported in *Literaturnaya Gazeta*, August 17, 1954.
43. *Oktyabr'*, No. 4, 1954, p. 118. Vershigora's words were: "The book is a striking example, undeserving of imitation, of bureaucratic, play-it-safe writing, which lacks the chief kernel of historical study—patriotism."
44. The resolution of the Presidium of the Board of the Union of Writers removing Panferov as editor of *Oktyabr'* was published in *Literaturnaya Gazeta*, June 5, 1954. Ten days earlier, A. Surkov, the head of the Writers Union had charged Panferov with "unworthy, antisocial acts" in a context that seemed to link him with the disgraced writers (*Pravda*, May 25, 1954).
45. A. M. Pankratova *et al* (eds.), *Istoriya SSSR, III*. The relevant page references are: 1948 (English) ed., p. 413; 1951 ed., p. 392; 1957 ed., p. 242.

Chapter 6—The Post-Stalin Reappraisal of the History of the War
(pp. 128–152)

1. *The 50th Anniversary of the Communist Party of the Soviet Union (1903–1953)* (New York, 1953), pp. 21–22.
2. Garthoff, *Soviet Strategy in the Nuclear Age* (New York, 1958), p. 156.
3. *Pravda*, March 13, 1954.
4. *Trud*, March 5, 1954. A commemorative article on Stalin contained the first of the revised "war records," of which various others were to be added in the next two years, listing only Khrushchev and Bulganin of the then collective leaders as having been among the Party leaders sent to the front during the war.
5. G. M. Malenkov, "32nd Anniversary of the Great October Socialist Revolution" (Moscow, 1949), p. 21.
6. "O roli vnezapnosti v sovremennoy voyne," *Voyennaya Mysl'*, No. 2, 1955.
7. Gen. V. Kurasov, *Krasnaya Zvezda*, April 27, 1958.
8. *Voyennaya Mysl'*, No. 3, 1955, pp. 7–8.
9. *Ibid.*, pp. 3–18.
10. *Ibid.*, p. 5.
11. *Ibid.*, pp. 7–8.
12. "Pobeda sovetskogo voyennogo iskusstva v velikoy otechestvennoy voyne," *Voyennaya Mysl'*, No. 5, 1955, p. 26.

13. *Ibid.*, pp. 22–23.
14. *Ibid.*, p. 32.
15. "O nekotorykh voprosakh sovetskoy voyennoy nauki," *Voyennaya Mysl'*, No. 3, 1955, p. 13.
16. *Ibid.*
17. *Literaturnaya Gazeta*, May 28, 1955.
18. *Ibid.*
19. *Ibid.*, June 2, 1955.
20. "O razrabotke i torii velikoy otechestvennoy voyny Sovetskogo soyuza," *Voprosy Istorii*, No. 5, 1955.
21. *Ibid.*, p. 8.
22. "Vnezapnost v istorii voyn," *Voyennyy Vestnik*, No. 11, 1955.
23. Tel'pukhovskiy *et al., op. cit.*
24. *Voprosy Istorii*, No. 2, 1956.
25. *Ibid.*, p. 202.
26. *Ibid.*, pp. 204–5, 210.
27. *Ibid.*, p. 204.
28. *Ibid.*, p. 205.
29. *Ibid.*, p. 209.
30. *Partinaya Zhizn*, No. 6, 1956, p. 20.
31. *Ibid.*, No. 7, 1956, p. 8.
32. *Pravda*, July 6, 1956.
33. *Leningradskaya Pravda*, July 27, 1956.
34. *Propagandist*, No. 8, 1956.
35. *Izvestiya*, April 27, 1956.
36. *Voyennyy Vestnik*, No. 4, 1956, condensed in *Current Digest of the Soviet Press*, May 30, 1956, pp. 3–4.
37. *Ibid.*, p. 4.
38. *Ibid.*
39. *Krasnaya Zvezda*, May 9, 1956, translated in *Current Digest of the Soviet Press*, June 13, 1956.
40. "XX s'ezd KPSS i zadachi issledovaniya istorii partii," *Voprosy Istorii*, No. 3, 1956. For the remarks on the history of the war, see p. 10.
41. *Voprosy Istorii*, No. 5, 1956.
42. *Ibid.*, p. 150.
43. V. Evstigneyev, P. Zhilin, S. Roginskiy, "Glubzhe izuchat' istoriyu velikoy otechestvennoy voyny," *Kommunist*, No. 10, 1956.
44. *Ibid.*, p. 64.
45. *Novyy Mir*, No. 12, 1956.
46. See pp. 57–60 of this work.
47. Simonov, *loc. cit.*, p. 246.
48. Maurice Friedberg, "The Background to the Third Congress of the Union of Soviet Writers," *Bulletin of the Institute for the Study of the USSR*, V, No. 12 (December, 1958), 38.
49. Granin's story appeared in *Novyy Mir*, No. 8, 1956. The others were all included in the anthology of the Moscow writers community, *Literaturnaya Moskva*, II, 1956.
50. *Moskva*, No. 4, 1957.

51. *Literaturnaya Gazeta,* August 31, 1957.
52. *Ibid.*
53. *Moskva,* No. 6, 1957.
54. *Novyy Mir,* Nos. 7, 8, 1957.
55. *Ibid.,* No. 7, 1957, pp. 60–61.
56. Quoted by Anatoliy Sofronov, *Literaturnaya Gazeta,* December 7, 1957.
57. *Zvaigzne,* No. 23, 1956.

Chapter 7—The Consolidation of the Post-Stalin Revisions
(pp. 153–175)

1. *Pravda,* February 23, 1957.
2. *Izvestiya,* February 23, 1957.
3. *Krasnaya Zvezda,* February 23, 1957.
4. *Ibid.,* May 9, 1957.
5. V. D. Vasilevskiy (ed.), *Boyevyye deystviya strelkovogo polka. Sbornik boyevykh primerov* (Moscow, 1958).
6. Examples of these translations are: *Itogi vtoroy mirovoy voyny* (Moscow, 1957), a translation of the German collection *Bilanz des zweiten Weltkriegs* (Hamburg, 1953); F. V. Mellentin, *Tankovyye srazheniya 1939–1945 gg. Boyevoe primeneniye tankov vo vtoroy mirovoy voyne* (Moscow, 1957), translated from the English edition of General von Mellenthin's work; *Mirovaya voyna 1939–1945 gody* (Moscow, 1957), a translation of the German *Weltkrieg 1939–1945* (Stuttgart, 1954); S. E. Morison, *Bitva za Atlantiku (sentyabr' 1939–may 1943).* *Istoriya morskikh operatsiy voyennomorskogo flota SShA vo vtoroy mirovoy voyne* (Moscow, 1956); F. S. Sherman, *Amerikanskiye avianostsy v voyne na Tikhom okeane* (Moscow, 1956); K. Tippelskirkh, *Istoriya vtoroy mirovoy voyny* (Moscow, 1956), a translation of *Geschichte des zweiten Weltkriegs* (Bonn, 1956).
7. Ya. Iosseliani, N. Milgram, *Izvestiya,* June 25, 1958.
8. *Istoriya velikoy otechestvennoy voyny sovetskogo soyuza,* I, 415–16. G. I. Kulik, named Deputy Commissar of Defense in 1939, was promoted to Marshal of the Soviet Union in 1940. His biography is not listed in the *Great Soviet Encyclopedia.* L. Z. Mekhlis (1885–1953) was Chief of the Main Political Administration of the Red Army from 1937 to 1940. He was named People's Commissar of State Control in September, 1940, and, according to the *Encyclopedia,* at the outset of the war was assigned to work in the Soviet Army. E. A. Shchadenko (1885–1951) held a number of posts, mainly in the political apparatus of the army during the prewar period. During the first years of the war, according to the *Encyclopedia,* he occupied "responsible offices in the central apparatus of the People's Commissariat of Defense."
9. *Ibid.,* II, 10. The charges against Zhukov and Timoshenko were publicized in the propaganda surrounding the twentieth anniversary of the Nazi invasion, which was commemorated in June, 1961. Cf. Eremenko's review of the second volume of the new official history of the war in *Krasnaya Zvezda,* June 20, 1961, and Platonov's review of the same book in the following issue.

10. *V pomoshch' politicheskomu samoobrazovaniyu*, No. 7, 1958, p. 19.
11. *Voyenno-istoricheskiy Zhurnal*, No. 3, 1960, p. 22.
12. *Ibid.*, p. 21.
13. *Ibid.*, p. 23.
14. A. M. Samsonov, *Stalingradskaya bitva ot oborony i otstupleniy k velikoy pobede na Volge: istoricheskiy ocherk* (Moscow, 1960), p. 66.
15. Cf. Platonov (ed.), *Vtoraya mirovaya voyna, 1939–1945 gg.: voyenno-istoricheskiy ocherk* (Moscow, 1958), pp. 176–79, and *Istoriya velikoy otechestvennoy voyny*, I, 473–79.
16. Platonov, *Vtoraya mirovaya voyna*, p. 186.
17. *Ibid.*, pp. 219–20.
18. *Istoriya velikoy*, I, 441.
19. *Ibid.*, II, 35.
20. Samsonov, *op. cit.*, pp. 127–28, 305. The latter passage is quoted from A. S. Zav'yalov, T. E. Kalyadin, *Bitva za kavkaz 1942–1943 gg.* (Moscow, 1957), one of a number of books on individual operatiɔns that have appeared over the last few years.
21. *Voyenno-istoricheskiy Zhurnal*, No. 2, 1960, p. 82.
22. Samsonov, *op. cit.*, p. 106.
23. *Voyenno-istoricheskiy Zhurnal*, No. 3, 1960, p. 36.
24. *Ibid.*, No. 2, 1960, p. 28.
25. *Ibid.*, p. 108.
26. Tel'pukhovskiy *et al.*, *op. cit.*, p. 25.
27. *Voprosy istorii*, No. 5, 1956, p. 150.
28. P. Derevyanko, D. Proyektor, "K voprosu o kharaktere vtoroy mirovoy voyny," *Kommunist*, No. 5, 1958.
29. E. Boltin, G. Deborin, "The Character of World War II," *World Marxist Review*, No. 9, 1959; introduction to *Istoriya velikoy otechestvennoy voyny*, I, xv-xxiii.
30. *Istoriya velikoy otechestvennoy voyny*, I, 152.
31. Deborin, *Vtoraya mirovaya voyna* (Moscow, 1958); *Istoriya Kommunisticheskoy partii sovetskogo soyuza* (Moscow, 1959); *Istoriya SSSR: epokha sotsializma* (Moscow, 1958).
32. *Voyenno-istoricheskiy Zhurnal*, No. 5, 1960, pp. 105, 107.
33. *Ibid.*, No. 8, 1960, p. 91.
34. V. Nekrasov, *V okopakh Stalingrada* (Moscow, 1955), p. 145. This book was published originally in 1946.
35. *Ibid.*, pp. 147–48.
36. Colonel A. Grylev, *Krasnaya Zvezda*, Feb. 14, 1962.
37. See p. 154 of this study.
38. Simonov, *Zhivyye i mertvyye*, (Moscow, 1960), p. 106.

Bibliography

This bibliography lists only those materials used directly in the preparation of this work. It is by no means a comprehensive list of materials relevant to the Soviet history of the war. Items not discussed in the text are annotated briefly.

PRIMARY SOURCES

Soviet Books and Pamphlets

ANISIMOV, I. V., and KUZMAN, G. V. *Velikaya otechestvennaya voyna Sovetskogo Soyuza, 1941–1945 gg.: kratkiy istoricheskiy ocherk.* Moscow, 1952.
Superficial and schematic.

AVARIN, V. YA. *Borba za Tikhiy okean; Yapono-Amerikanskiye protivorechiya.* Moscow, 1947.

———. *Bor'ba za Tikhiy okean; agressiya SShA i Anglii, ikh protivorechiya, i osvoboditel'naya bor'ba narodov.* Moscow, 1952.

BURDZHALOV, E. *Velikaya otechestvennaya voyna Sovetskogo Soyuza, 1941–1945 gg. Lektsii prochitannyye v Vysshey Partinoy Shkole pri TsK KPSS.* Moscow, 1953.
A propaganda tract.

DEBORIN, G. A. *Vtoraya mirovaya voyna.* Moscow, 1958.
Focuses on the diplomatic history of the war. Despite the relatively recent date of publication, this book shows no historiographical progress from the traditional propaganda fare of the Stalinist period.

EREMENKO, A. I. *Protiv fal'sifikatsii istorii vtoroy mirovoy voyny.* Moscow, 1958.
A hard-hitting attack on a number of the more notable German accounts of the war.

———. *Stalingrad.* Moscow, 1961.
A firsthand account of the Stalingrad battle by the commander of the Stalingrad Front. A very valuable historical source both for the factual information it provides and for Eremenko's observations and judgments. It is also interesting as a political phenomenon since it carries the praise of Khrushchev's wartime role to unprecedented heights.

GOLIKOV, S. *Vydayushchiyesya pobedy Sovetskoy armii v velikoy otechest-vennoy voyne, 1941–1945.* Leningrad, 1952.
Intended for secondary and trade schools. Popular and inspirational. A second amplified and revised edition was brought out in 1954.

GROSSMAN, VASILIY. *The Years of the War.* Moscow: Foreign Languages Publishing House, 1946.

INSTITUT ISTORII, AKADEMIYA NAUK SSSR. *Trudy po novoy i noveyshey istorii.* Vol. I. Moscow, 1948.

INSTITUT MARKSIZMA-LENINIZMA PRI TSK KPSS. *Istoriya Velikoy otechest-vennoy voyny Sovetskogo Soyuza 1941–1945.* Vols. I–III. Moscow, 1960–61.
This is the official history of the war. Three more volumes are still to be published. Despite the bias of its interpretations, it represents a genuine contribution to the historical record of the Soviet-German war.

IVASHIN, I. F. *Mezhdunarodnyye otnosheniya i vneshnyaya politika SSSR v period vtoroy mirovoy voyny. Lektsii prochitannyye v Vysshey partiynoy shkole pri TSK KPSS.* Moscow, 1954.
Extremely doctrinaire treatment of the policies of the Allies during the war.

KULISH, V. M. *Vtoroy front.* Moscow, 1960.
A professional military analysis of the Allied invasion of Europe. Notable for the virtual absence of propaganda interpretations or political moralizing.

LAN, V. *SShA ot pervoy do vtoroy mirovoy voyny.* Moscow, 1947.

MINTS, I. I. *Velikaya otechestvennaya voyna Sovetskogo Soyuza.* Moscow, 1947.

NEKRASOV, V. *V okopakh Stalingrada.* Moscow, 1955.

PLATONOV, S. P. (ed.). *Vtoraya mirovaya voyna, 1939–1945 gg.: voyenno-istoricheskiy ocherk.* Moscow, 1958.
The best Soviet single-volume history of the war.

POTEMKIN, V. P. *et al.* (eds.). *Istoriya diplomatii. Vol. III: Diplomatiya v period podgotovki vtoroy mirovoy voyny (1919–1939 gg.).* Moscow, 1945.

Sbornik materialov po istorii Sovetskogo voyennogo iskusstva v velikoy otechestvennoy voyne, 1941–1945 gg. (Frunze Military Academy). Moscow, 1956.
Contains a collection of articles on various phases of the war taken from such sources as *Military Thought.*

Sbornik materialov po istorii voyennogo iskusstva v velikoy otechestvennoy voyne. 4 vols. and 1 vol. of maps (Voroshilov Military Academy). Moscow, 1955.
Arranged on the same principles as the book listed immediately above.

SIMONOV, KONSTANTIN. *Days and Nights.* Translated by JOSEPH BARNES. New York, 1945.

———. *Zhivyye i mertvyye.* Moscow, 1960.

SHILOVSKIY, E. A. *Razgrom nemetskikh voysk pod Moskvoy.* Moscow, 1943.

STALIN, I. V. *O velikoy otechestvennoy voyne Sovetskogo Soyuza* (5th ed.). Moscow, 1949.

————. "Speech Delivered by J. V. Stalin at a Meeting of Voters of the Stalin Electoral Area of Moscow, February 9, 1946," *Information Bulletin*, Embassy of the U.S.S.R. Washington, D.C., March, 1946.

Strategy and Tactics of the Soviet German War, by Officers and Soviet War Correspondents. London, 1942.

Despite the high authority of a number of the authors, such as Rokossovskiy, Eremenko, *et al.*, most of the articles are of a propagandistic nature, and none deals with strategy proper.

TEL'PUKHOVSKIY, B. S. *Vsemirno-istoricheskoye znacheniye pobedy SSSR v velikoy otechestvennoy voyne. Stenogramma publichnoy lektsii prochitannoy v Moskve.* Moscow, 1952.

A brief summary of the political "lessons" of the war, narrowly interpreted according to Stalinist criteria.

————. *Velikaya pobeda Sovetskoy armii pod Stalingradom.* Moscow, 1953.

Stalin's "constantly operating factors" are described as the basic key to understanding the Soviet victory. Stalin liberally quoted.

————. *Velikaya otechestvennaya voyna Sovetskogo Soyuza 1941–1945; kratkiy ocherk.* Moscow, 1959.

Essentially a revised version of the book listed immediately below.

————. *et al.* (eds.). *Ocherki istorii velikoy otechestvennoy voyny sovetskogo Soyuza, 1941–1945 gg.* Moscow, 1955.

The first full-scale history of the war published under professional historical auspices. Generally reflects the moderate level of revision achieved before the major revisionary movement of 1955 had gotten under way. Consistent effort made throughout to play up the role of the people by endless accounts of heroism, etc. Commanding officers identified for all major operations.

TOLCHENOV, M. P. *Amerikano-Angliiskiye fal'sifikatory istorii vtoroy mirovoy voyny.* Moscow, 1953.

SOVIET INFORMATION BUREAU. *Falsificators of History (an historical note).* Moscow, 1948.

U.S.S.R. MINISTRY OF FOREIGN AFFAIRS. *Documents and Materials Relating to the Eve of the Second World War.* New York, 1948.

Velikaya otechestvennaya voyna Sovetskogo Soyuza. Materialy po chetvertoy teme. Moscow, 1948.

VERSHIGORA, P. *Men With a Clear Conscience.* Moscow: Foreign Languages Publishing House, 1949.

VOROB'YEV, F. D., and KRAVTSOV, V. M. *Pobedy Sovetskikh vooruzhennykh sil v velikoy otechestvennoy voyne, 1941–1945 gg.; kratkiy ocherk.* Moscow, 1954.

This is one of the better early post-Stalin histories. It can still be used for a factual check against other Soviet accounts. For example, it contains one of the rare reference in Soviet sources to Zhukov's role as coordinator of the defense of Stalingrad.

ZAMYATIN, N. *Desyat' sokrushitel'nykh udarov; kratkiy obzor operatsiy krasnoy armii v 1944 g.* Moscow, 1945.

ZUBOK, L. I. *Noveyshaya istorii, 1918–1939 gg.* Moscow, 1948.

Soviet Newspapers and Periodicals

Bolshevik
International Relations
Izvestiya
Krasnaya Zvezda
Kommunist
Literaturnaya Gazeta
Novyy Mir
Oktyabr'
Pravda
Voprosy Istorii
Voyennaya Mysl'
Voyennyy Vestnik
Voyenno-istoricheskiy Zhurnal
VOKS Bulletin
Znamya
Zvezda

Translations of and Guides to Soviet Materials

Current Digest of the Soviet Press
Knizhnaya letopis'
Information Bulletin. Embassy of the U.S.S.R., Vols. 1–12. Washington, D.C., 1941–52.
Soviet Monitor. A Tass publication. London, 1945–50.
U.S. FEDERAL COMMUNICATIONS COMMISSION. *Transcripts of Short-Wave Broadcasts: Moscow.* Washington, D.C., 1941.
Vsemirno-istoricheskaya pobeda Sovetskogo Soyuza v velikoy otechestvennoy voyne; rekomendatel'nyy ukazatel' literatury. Moscow, 1950.

SECONDARY SOURCES

ALEXANDROVA, VERA. "The Russian People and the 'Lost Peace'—in Literature," *Modern Review*, No. 7–8, January, 1949.
ALLEN, W. E. D. *The Russian Campaigns of 1941–1943.* London: Cambridge University Press, 1944.
BARGHOORN, FREDERICK C. *The Soviet Image of the United States: A Study in Distortion.* New York: Harcourt, Brace and Company, 1950.
BELOFF, MAX. *Soviet Policy in the Far East, 1944–1951.* London and New York: Oxford University Press, 1953.
BLAU, GEORGE E. *The German Campaign in Russia: Planning and Operations, 1940–1942.* (Department of the Army Study.) Washington, D.C., 1955.
CASSIDY, HENRY CLARENCE. *Moscow Dateline 1941–1943.* London, 1943.
COUNTS, GEORGE S., and LODGE, NUCIA. *The Country of the Blind.* Boston, 1949.
CHURCHILL, WINSTON S. *The Second World War.* 6 vols. Boston: Houghton Mifflin Company, 1948–53.

DEPARTMENT OF MILITARY ART AND ENGINEERING, THE UNITED STATES MILITARY ACADEMY. *The War in Eastern Europe (June, 1941–May, 1945)*, West Point, N.Y., 1952.

DINERSTEIN, H. S. *War and the Soviet Union: Nuclear Weapons and the Revolution in Soviet Military and Political Thinking*. New York: Frederick A. Praeger, 1959.

———, and GOURÉ, LEON. *Two Studies in Soviet Controls: Communism and the Russian Peasant; Moscow in Crisis*. With a Foreword by PHILIP E. MOSELY. Chicago: The Free Press of Glencoe, 1955.

FISCHER, GEORGE. *Soviet Opposition to Stalin: A Case Study in World War II*. Cambridge, Mass.: Harvard University Press, 1952.

FULLER, J. F. C. *The Second World War, 1939–1945: A Strategical and Tactical History*. New York: Duell, Sloan & Pearce, 1949.

GAFENCU, GRIGOIRE. *The Last Days of Europe: A Diplomatic Diary*. Translated by E. FLETCHER ALLEN. New Haven, Conn.: Yale University Press, 1948.

GARTHOFF, RAYMOND L. *Soviet Military Doctrine*. Chicago: The Free Press of Glencoe, 1953.

———. *Soviet Strategy in the Nuclear Age*. Rev. ed. New York: Frederick A. Praeger, 1962.

GOERLITZ, WALTER. *History of the German General Staff, 1657–1945*. Translated by BRIAN BATTERSHAW. With an Introduction by WALTER MILLIS. New York: Frederick A. Praeger, 1953.

GUDERIAN, HEINZ. *Panzer Leader*. Translated by CONSTANTINE FITZGIBBON. With a Foreword by B. H. LIDDELL HART. New York: E. P. Dutton & Company, 1952.

GUILLAUME, AUGUSTIN. *Soviet Arms and Soviet Power: The Secrets of Russia's Might*. Washington, 1949.

KASÉ, TODSHIKAZU. *Journey to the Missouri*. New Haven, Conn.: Yale University Press, 1949.

KERR, WALTER B. *The Russian Army: Its Men, Its Leaders, Its Battles*. New York, 1944.

LIDDELL HART, B. H. (ed.). *The Soviet Army—1946 to the Present*. New York: Harcourt, Brace and Company, 1956.

MAGIDOFF, ROBERT. *The Kremlin vs. the People*. New York, 1953.

MANSTEIN, ERICH VON. *Lost Victories*. Translated by ANTHONY G. POWELL. With a Foreword by B. H. LIDDELL HART. Chicago: Henry Regnery Company, 1958.

MELLENTIN, F. V. (MELLENTHIN, F. W. VON). *Tankovyye srazheniya 1939–1945 gg.; boyevoe primeneniye tankov vo vtoroy mirovoy voyne*, ed. A. P. PANFILOV. Translated by P. N. VIDUETSKIY and V. I. SAVVIN. Moscow, 1957.

Mirovaya Voyna 1939–1945 gody. Translated by A. A. VYSOKOVSKIY and A. I. D'YAKONOV. Moscow, 1957.

NICOLAEVSKIY, BORIS I. (ed.). "The Crimes of the Stalin Era, Special Report to the 20th Congress of the Communist Party of the Soviet Union, by Nikita S. Khrushchev," *New Leader*, Supplement, 1956.

ROSSI, A. *The Russo-German Alliance*. London, 1950.

SONTAG, RAYMOND J., and BEDDIE, JAMES S. (eds.). *Nazi-Soviet Relations, 1939–1941*. Washington, 1948.

U.S. DEPARTMENT OF DEFENSE. *The Entry of the Soviet Union into the War Against Japan: Military Plans 1941–1945*. Washington, D.C., 1955.

United States Strategic Bombing Survey. Japan's Struggle to End the War. Washington, 1946.

WEINBERG, GERHARD L. *Germany and the Soviet Union, 1939–1941*. Leiden, 1954.

WERTH, ALEXANDER. *The Year of Stalingrad*. New York, 1947.

WOLFE, BERTRAM D. *Khrushchev and Stalin's Ghost: Text, Background, and Meaning of Khrushchev's Secret Report to the Twentieth Congress on the Night of February 24–25, 1956*. New York: Frederick A. Praeger, 1957.

Index